A Let

Son –

a carer's perspective on community care in the 21st century

Gill Holt

chipmunkapublishing
the mental health publisher

Published by
Chipmunkapublishing
United Kingdom

http://www.chipmunkapublishing.com

Copyright © 2020 Gill Holt

ISBN   978-1-78382-550-9

A Letter to Alex

I found it easiest to recount my experience of my son's illness in the form of a letter to him. For large parts of the development of the illness, my husband and I had to guess what was happening and what he was thinking since he often would not – sometimes could not – articulate his feelings and plans, and so this format allows me to open up questions through conversations with him. A happy by-product of this approach allowed me to imagine sometimes that I still was really talking with him.

The names of all mental health professionals and hospital wards have been changed.

Gill Holt

Foreword

This book is valuable in describing, from a carer's perspective, a ten-year development in the awful illness of schizophrenia, a disease that tends to develop in late teens or early twenties. It demonstrates how difficult it is for parents to detect symptoms, discover what they may mean, and – most importantly – know how to go about getting help. As such, it should help community-based health practitioners to identify patients presenting with such afflictions, and how best to support their families in securing clinical and social support.

But it also describes how ill-resourced our mental health system is to deal with it, when compared with other life-threatening diseases such as cancer, heart disease and diabetes. In 2016 the Government's Mental Health Taskforce Strategy revealed that, while 'mental health accounts for 23% of NHS activity, NHS spending on secondary mental health services is equivalent to just half of this'.

So, I believe that this book could make an important contribution in two ways:
- Demonstrating to politicians and policy-makers that they need to be sure that the reported increase in funding for mental health services is actually reaching its intended target at local level
- Help professionals in the health service – in both primary and secondary care, and in mental and physical care, since all are inherently inter-related – to deliver the best service they can, informed by the experience of carers and supporting family members.

There is much material in this book from which students in health professions can learn about real experiences; and also for those already practicing in community or hospital settings. As such, I think it would be a helpful inclusion in reading lists for university and college students in medical, health and social care professions, and also provide case study material for the many continuing professional development training programmes in this field.

Dr Angela Baird GP
with 30 years' experience in general practice and out-of-hours urgent care.

Chapters

1. Prologue – 13th June 2013

2. Early Signs? – April 1983 to September 2002

3. University shutdown – September 2002 to May 2006

4. The Breakdown – 31st May 2006

5. Early Intervention – June 2006 to 2007

6. I Just Need a Job   - June 2007 to March 2009

7. Home and Away, a Revolving Door – March 2009 to August 2011

8. Sectioned and Privatised   - September 2011 to June 2012

9. New Friends? – July 2012 to February 2013

10. A Month in the Life – February to May 2013

11. Window of Opportunity – May 2013 to December 2013

12. Missed Opportunity – 11th December 2013 to 2nd January 2014

13. Epilogue – Sweet Child of Mine

Gill Holt

A Letter to My Son

1.   Prologue – 13th June 2013

It was very pleasant, ahead of the full glare of the June sun in the Portuguese Algarve. We four tennis players, used to rain, frost and worse at our club in Sheffield, had enjoyed our game from eight thirty to ten, and were looking forward to the reward of an al fresco breakfast back at Jackie's house in Varandas do Lago.

As I walked into the house I picked up a text from Dad "Just tried to ring but couldn't get through – ring me urgently x." My friends busied themselves with making breakfast while I went into the garden in search of a decent signal for a phone call, dread seeping into every pore. "Hi, it's me, what's the problem?"

"I'm afraid that yesterday I found Alex in bed semi-conscious, and he is in the Northern General. He's overdosed again and this time it seems he was sick and inhaled his own vomit so has developed pneumonia. He is in a critical condition in Intensive Care, and I think you need to come home". Something deep inside seemed to be turning somersaults. How many times had you tried to end your life but without success? You'd never got as far as Intensive Care. All I could find to say was "Oh no....", swallow, deep breath..."Right, I'll let you know when I can get there."

There was a Ryan Air flight from Faro to Manchester which had seats available, but I was unable to book online, and had to head off immediately for the airport if I was to catch it. My friends packed my case while I relayed this information to Dad, who said he would organise a taxi to take me direct from Manchester airport to the hospital in Sheffield. Minutes later we were all in the car en route to the airport. My mind was completely scrambled as I fretted over what I might find when I arrived back in Sheffield, around four or five hours from now. I had never been so far away on the previous distressing occasions.

My friends stayed with me as long as they could to keep me company. However, once on my own in the departure lounge, my nerves were really jangling. Dad rang with the taxi arrangements and also gave me a direct line to Intensive Care if I wanted to speak with the charge nurse. This I did, but all she could do was confirm what I already knew – that your condition was very serious but currently stable. At some stage, in my agitated state, I managed to lose my boarding pass, arriving at the gate without it, and unsure of the consequences. However, I just had to wait to be the last person to board before they would let me through, and it was OK.

Safely on board I had two and a half hours to contemplate what was happening to you. After seven years of experience with your illness, of worrying our way through numerous stressful incidents and crises, and managing to get you (and us) through it, if this was to be the end of it all how would we cope? How could we engineer a life without you? I have never made such a dreadful journey. Arriving in Manchester I was grateful to find the taxi driver easily, but became increasingly edgy as we made our way to Sheffield. Should I ring Dad to see how things were, in advance of arriving? I decided against that. An hour and a half later I entered the Intensive Care Unit not knowing whether I would find a very poorly – or a deceased – Alex. Fortunately it was the former.

The scene inside the unit was quite amazing. I was introduced to your room by a young nurse who explained that you were still at risk as your temperature was still at a dangerous level, and so all their efforts were focused on reducing it. You were naked, smothered in ice packs and connected to machines by all sorts of wires, with Dad watching on. We hugged. The nurse said your temperature had stabilised during the day and also had occasionally dipped, which was a good sign, but that you were not out of danger yet.

Dad took me through the turn of events that led to your predicament, unfortunately a reasonably familiar scenario to us over the last few years. How did our lovely and talented son come to this pass? What had happened to you?

2. Early Signs? – 1983 to 2002

One of the singular cruelties of your condition was that you were not born with it. So, rather than growing up with a familiar set of symptoms – however distressing – and getting used to dealing with them, your illness crept into your (and our) life in an insidious fashion, just at the time when you should have been looking forward to a fulfilling life ahead – adolescence. From midway through secondary school there were occasions when you displayed perverse or negative behaviour, and chose to be less sociable than previously, but didn't that often happen through adolescence? In retrospect, I now know that in fact you were even then hearing those malevolent voices, constantly taunting you and undermining your self-respect; and they were to wreak a devastating effect on the development of the gentle, affectionate boy you had been.

24th April 1983
Hard to believe that just three days ago I vowed that I would never have another child after my eighteen-hour ordeal in the labour ward. The nurse announced that you had the biggest head delivered yet that year – and didn't I know it! A large baby, born two weeks late on the Queen's birthday, everyone on the ward had said you already looked six months old, but lying there on our sheepskin rug when we first arrived home from the hospital, you looked so fragile and dependent, we could feel the weight of responsibility growing within us – and it was sweet.

You were a demanding baby, needing much feeding and stimulation and taking little sleep, but oh what a delightful infant and young boy you became ... but I would say that, wouldn't I? When your brother came along you showed some jealousy for a while, but soon settled down into creating of him a small playmate and companion. You and Matthew gave much joy to your grandparents, particularly to my parents, for whom you were then their only grandchildren – although neither of them would live to see either of you fully grown. You would probably remember those Saturday trips to Liverpool, Alex, to see my parents, and half-terms in

Grange-over-Sands, to spend time with Dad's parents; but not those beautiful first daily walks the three of us – you, Matthew and I – made to Forge Dam through Whiteley Woods, when we first moved to Sheffield and before I found a job, you trotting alongside the buggy, full of anticipation of shooting down the big slide in the playground and enjoying a milkshake in the café?

We soon developed a busy, full life as a family. Dad and I both worked full time, and I travelled out of town, so a nanny, Catherine, looked after you during the day. But we all enjoyed bedtime reading on weekdays, and weekends brimming with outings and pursuing an ever-changing range of hobbies, interspersed with lovely family holidays and half-term trips to visit grandparents. For thirteen or fourteen years we had a charmed life. There is no way that Dad and I could have imagined the troubles – no, the torture – that you (and us with you) would have to endure in the coming years.

Such a bright and inquisitive boy, and a great reader, you developed swiftly all the necessary skills through early years at school, becoming one of their star pupils, particularly gifted in both maths and creative writing. You and Matthew had extensive friendship groups and Dad and I felt really blessed in having such a happy young family, full of hopes for the future, and oblivious to the awful development – the random cruelty – which would undermine your progress to a successful adult life.

You developed an early passion for football, learning the ropes at Saturday training sessions at the local playing fields, and then playing for Sheffield Redmires in the Sunday league for six or seven years – remember all those cold Sunday mornings on windswept slopes around the hills of Sheffield? Although we moved from Merseyside when you were only three, you saw the wisdom of following my lead in supporting Liverpool FC as being a more rewarding prospect than either of the local teams. However, Sheffield Wednesday was in the Premier League then, so when Liverpool travelled over from across the Pennines, we all went to watch them play. One year Dad was given, through work, hospitality tickets for the last match of the year at

Anfield, and I can still remember the level of excitement you displayed as you set off in the car. You returned home absolutely full of it, clutching the autographs of some of the players whom you had been able to meet afterwards. An obsession with Liverpool FC was to be one of the few interests that managed to survive your future personality metamorphosis.

Then there were your three years as a chorister at St. John's Church. You were prompted to join, rather late, when you found that Matthew and his friend Philip, who had just started at aged eight, were augmenting their pocket money with the (albeit small) allowance from the church – and enjoying the bonuses available for singing at weddings on Saturdays! How lovely it was to see you both singing in the choir at Ripon Cathedral once on a choir exchange weekend; even better to watch you sing a solo on various occasions at St. John's; and a final climax to your choir exploits – you and Matthew chosen to sing the first verse of 'Once in Royal David's City' as a duet, in candlelight, to open the Christmas Eve midnight mass. This delighted your grandad, who was present, and I'm sure he would have enjoyed as much, had he been able to hear it, the duet of 'God be in my Head' you sang together at his funeral only three months later.

You changed gradually from a shy, gentle, intelligent and affectionate boy into a moody and challenging teenager, but there was really nothing to distinguish your behaviour from many of your friends and peers, in tune with a fairly wide male adolescent trend at that time – beginning to under-achieve at school and intent on resisting parental guidance. Were you the only one who refused to attend the careers evening at school to help in selection of A levels? Was there anything seriously worrying about my being called in to school after you had thrown a pot of yoghurt over a girl at the dinner table? Should I have enquired further when I was joking with your friend, Ben, one Friday night that you always seemed to keep your friends waiting in the hall before going out for the night and he said "Yes, but that's just Alex – he has his own way?" And was your explanation plausible as to why you shaved off all your lovely shoulder-length hair the day before we were going to the open day at Leeds University?

So often I have reflected on this list of perverse behaviour, considered now in retrospect – how it could be consistent with what you told me later – that you started hearing voices at the age of around fifteen or sixteen. If we had known – if you could have told us – I have to think we could have found help to stop things developing further. Surely, as with cancer, early diagnosis dictates a greater chance of successful treatment and recovery? As it is, you suffered in silence, and we proceeded in ignorance. And so – in that ignorance – we were just delighted when you achieved the A level grades you needed to study joint honours in Psychology and Philosophy at Leeds University, and were supportive of your plan to spend a gap year, first, in Australia.

You worked flat-out at the lighting department in John Lewis seven days a week from July to Christmas to fund your travel. You really enjoyed it, made a new set of friends and – we found out later – made quite an impression generally. Your flight was booked for the beginning of February, and so you found another earning activity through January to top up your savings – driving a van round the north of England with your friend Tom selling posters on university campuses. You were the leader in the enterprise, frequently having to get Tom out of bed to set off in the early hours. You were pleased that you had a place at Leeds University having seen and been unimpressed with various other campuses. However, one morning, before setting off to work, I had to wake you up, and – in retrospect – I wonder if what happened next was a sign of some growing anxiety within you? As I said your name and nudged you awake, you cried sharply "Mum" as you reached up and grasped my arms tightly with wide open – and I felt, also, frightened – eyes. You insisted that no, you hadn't had a nightmare and yes, you were fine. But were you? Looking back, I think this was the first indication that all might not be well with you, a precursor to an emerging picture which would develop over the subsequent months. But it was the first of what would be the default response to our queries about your well-being –

"I'm fine, Mum." If you were hearing voices then, Alex, I wish – oh how I wish – you could have told us.

And then there was your laid back approach to catching the plane that would take you to Australia. It was an afternoon flight from Heathrow, and we wanted to leave sufficient time for any problems on the M1 en route. The night before you had set out all that you needed for your backpack, but that morning you were very slow in packing it all in. At the time we should have been leaving you were sitting in the hall playing your guitar casually, next to a half-packed bag. Was this reluctance to get on with it a last-minute anxiety about whether this experience was really for you? However, you did get on that plane, and I can still see the image of you going through the departures door with backpack and guitar, and thinking that my lovely 18-year-old son was setting off on his own to go to the other side of the world for eight months. I realised how much I was going to miss you. I felt bereft and cried for the first part of the journey home, but managed to regain control of my feelings by starting to plan a visit to Australia so that we could see you there. If I timed it well it would only be four or five months before I would see you again!

We had bought you a new mobile phone so that we could keep in contact while you were away. You had promised to ring from Bangkok to let us know you had arrived safely, once you had settled in to the hostel in which the company through which you had organised your trip had block-booked rooms for you and about ten other fellow travellers for a 'stop-over' – but, of course, you didn't ring, and we could not get through to you. I imagined all sorts of dreadful possibilities – as I had when two years earlier you had failed to contact us immediately on your arrival at the end of your first solo trip, at seventeen, to Ireland with friends. But we had to wait three more days until you had moved on and arrived in the hostel in Sydney before we managed to speak. You sounded happy though, and had made friends with some of the others in the group, sufficient to find shared accommodation with three or four of them. You settled first in a house near Bondi Beach, and later moved to one at Manly Beach, and it all seemed idyllic from our perspective.

While you worked to begin with to top up your funds, we had an agreed weekly phone conversation early on Saturday mornings – Saturday evening for you. It was exciting to hear of your exploits, swimming among exotic fish and weekend camping trips where you would share the site with kangaroos and huge monitor lizards. The regular phone slot continued when you set off backpacking up the east coast with two friends, and we had agreed to meet up with you in Cairns for a week on the beach, which I had planned as the high spot of our four-week holiday.

In our third week of travels, just as we pulled up our hire-car outside the Cairns hostel, there you were, coming out of the front door and turning in to the shop next door. It had been only four and a half months but somehow you looked significantly more mature than your nineteen years, with a confident swagger, deep tan and designer stubble! However, you exhibited no clue about the underlying anxiety you must have had in knowing that you had lost your passport and other valuables several days before. I had to raise the subject.

"Are you sure you haven't lost anything important, Alex?"

"Well yes, actually, I've left my passport somewhere, and can't track it down."

"Good news on that score – I had a call two days ago from the hostel in Byron Bay, saying that another traveller had found a pouch under the bed with your passport and bank card in it. He's going to post them to the hotel where we are all spending the next week, so you'll be so glad that I insisted, while you were away, that you leave a note of my phone number in your wallet, just in case you lost your phone and could not remember it! How long was it going to be before you mentioned this?"

We all laughed.

As we drove up the coast along the beautiful Captain Cook Highway towards Port Douglas, we heard about your experiences in places like Byron Bay, the Whitsunday Islands, and Fraser Island, and we enjoyed our week with you in a resort hotel on one of those glittering white Queensland beaches, snorkeling off the Barrier Reef, and driving to Cape Tribulation along a road where the rainforest meets the beach. But you did like to spend quite a bit of time on your own – in the hotel room, enjoying the facilities after weeks of basic hostels, or at the Internet café in Port Douglas. Was this just a natural function of your age and situation or were you already developing an aptitude to withdraw from company?

I think I remember Dad and I having a conversation about whether it was reasonable that you should seem so reclusive after not seeing us for so long. We both had concerns, but they were at such a different level to the anxiety and stress we were to experience later that they have receded into my memory bank. Again, in retrospect, on your return to Sheffield you were not exactly forthcoming with information about your eight-month experience. However, we had only a week before we would be taking you up to Leeds, and preparing for this took all our energies.

3. University Shut-down – September 2002 to May

2006

On your return from Australia we were all taken up with organising your move to Leeds. You seemed excited and all doubts about your well-being were sidelined. This was to be the beginning of your independence, and I was quietly reassured that, working at Leeds University myself, I could keep an eye on you should you have any problems. That reassurance was, however, ill-founded. In fact, your university years would push you over the edge into a cruel and debilitating illness. Things really started to develop once you started at university: growing difficulties with socialisation became evident; there were signs of anxiety or sometimes an apparent distractedness; and you were to make significant errors of judgement. And Dad and I were to experience how limited our influence would now be, when we didn't understand what was happening to you, you were secretive about it, you were over thirty miles away, and the University's confidentiality requirements made it difficult for us to intervene to good effect. Worst of all, your communication with us was increasingly brittle and sometimes angry.

One Saturday morning in late September 2002 we joined the long tail of cars making their way around Leeds city centre to the two adjacent universities in the city. Arriving at the brand-new student residence block, and unloading your belongings into the small studio flat, you were embarking on a new phase in your life, and we were full of expectations about where it might lead. It was good fun stocking up on household goods at the local hardware store, and we felt the buzz of all the new students filling up the area as we headed for a pub lunch in Headingly. I worked at the university, and a few days later you and a friend, whom you had, coincidentally, met in Australia, called in to the office after enrolling on your courses. How happy you seemed, bursting into the room.

"We've just been to register and thought we'd say hello. This is Caroline, my friend from Australia." You had travelled around Australia with two girls, one of whom, by coincidence, was also starting a degree at Leeds.

"Hello Caroline, Alex has talked about you a lot – what subject are you taking?"

"Biochemistry", she smiled.

"And how did you enjoy your time in Australia?"

"It was a great experience, thank you, and the scenery was just amazing."

"Alex tells me that he travelled up the coast with you and Gemma – I trust he behaved himself?"

She laughed "Well, he's not very good at getting up in the morning and once we had to leave him behind in the hostel or we'd have missed our bus, but he caught up with us the next day!"

You had to interject with "Well, actually, I chose to have an extra day in Byron Bay, as it was great swimming there."

And so this banter continued for a while, and I thought what a lovely, bubbly girl she was, how well you seemed to get on and I hoped that you would be able to remain friends.

During the first term at Leeds you called into the office on several occasions asking for advice on washing and cooking, and we started a habit of meeting for tea after work every couple of weeks. However, it was not long before negative aspects emerged. Driving you home to Sheffield for the weekend one Friday evening you explained how you really were not getting on with the others in the immediate vicinity in your flat. I was really surprised at this – you had always been such a popular boy at school with a wide friendship group, and our house had been a regular meeting place for the group to get together. Why should it have been different at university?

"Most of the people who live on my floor are not like me at all."

"What do you mean, not like you?"

"Well, they're loud and arrogant. They seem to have a lot of money and like throwing it around – 'Hooray Henries'. And they don't seem particularly interested in their courses."

"Surely they can't all be like that?" I asked, regretting my decision to register Alex in the brand new – and most expensive – hall of residence.

"Well, mostly."

"OK, well if it continues to be difficult there, concentrate on people on your course – they should have things in common with you, and they may even wish to share a rented house or flat for later in the year."
You continued to give details of nights out you had spent with them, and how uncomfortable they had made you feel, and I did experience a spike of anxiety – linking this conversation with your apparent tendency to seek solitude on our Australian holiday.

However, you took my advice and moved into a rented flat later in the year, but one day you came into my office and announced "Mum, I've been thinking that maybe I'm not cut out for university."
"Don't think that, just because you can't get on with everyone – lots of people have that problem. Anyway, what would you do instead? You haven't yet decided how you'd like to make a living – or have you now?"
"No, I haven't, but I've been thinking law maybe?"
We then had a conversation about the breadth of opportunities that could be available to you with a degree, compared to those without, and you agreed it would be a good idea to continue. But now I wonder if that was the first fatal mistake – a clue to your underlying anxiety that I failed to notice as hugely significant? Maybe university life was beginning to exacerbate the anxiety that in retrospect we found out you had already been experiencing, having heard occasional voices in your head for some years; an anxiety that we failed to recognise perhaps because of your habitual outwardly confident demeanour. I would hear later, ironically from your friend Caroline, that her (doctor) father had explained to her that often serious mental illness develops to the stage where it starts to become evident only when the sufferer starts to have to manage without parental support – so, often, at university. Why did we not know what was happening? I am sure that with a serious physical illness – cancer or diabetes, for instance – we would have detected any symptoms and known how to seek help.

In the first summer vacation you had a temporary job in an insurance office. I had organised what we thought might be our last family holiday, a treat in Cuba, to celebrate my fiftieth birthday. You – as did we all – obviously found the experience in that unusual country interesting, and we had a really enjoyable time. However, there were at times some signs of mildly unusual behaviour, hard to describe and harder to define – a certain 'twitchiness', perhaps? You would dart off on your own occasionally without any warning, and lose track of, or interest in, the subject in mid-conversation. Again I would learn from Caroline, after we'd lost you, that she and your other friends had also experienced this trait in your company, but put it down to a little eccentricity.

On our return from Cuba we had a big birthday party, which you clearly enjoyed with all your friends and cousins present. You and your friends danced with me and you danced with your Gran, and it was a typically sociable family occasion. We did not know then that it would be the last such event we would enjoy without the growing undercurrent of anxiety over your well-being.

A week after taking you back to Leeds to a new flat for the second year, there was a thunderbolt from the blue. Sitting at my desk at the university, I picked up a call from (an extremely agitated) Dad.
"I've just opened a letter which I assumed was for me but turned out to be for Alex. It was from the University confirming that he is no longer registered as a student! It seems he has failed a mandatory subject, taken a re-sit in the summer and failed again, so could not progress to the second year. What's going on, Gill? You've got to get hold of him!"
This was astonishing – we knew nothing of this – how could you think we would not find out, and how do you think we would feel when we did? It seems incredible, now, Alex, that you could have let this shocking news just emerge without any warning or explanation. What could have prompted you to believe that this was reasonable behaviour? This was the beginning of another worrying trend in your development – declining judgement in how to deal with significant issues and relationships.

Following a frantic phone call, we met in the student union café and discussed the situation over lunch. "Alex, why didn't you tell us you were having difficulty with your course – I asked you about it often enough?"

"Mum, I didn't want to worry you and thought I could deal with it."

"But what was it you found so difficult – you've never failed an exam before, never had any problems with school work?"

"Well, you see, I didn't like Psychology, so changed my course to Philosophy and Economics, but for that you needed A level maths."

"But you didn't do maths,"

"I know, but I thought that I could cope with it, and it was that I failed."

"But why didn't you tell us about the change, or about the re-sit – you know Dad could have helped you study?" (Andy had an Economics and Econometrics degree, and his favourite subject was maths). By this time there were tears welling up in your eyes, and I tried to give you a hug, but you wouldn't accept it. I had not seen you cry since you were thirteen when your cat was run over and killed. There was no point in asking any more 'whys', we had to look forward now. "OK, so what do you intend to do?"

"I've started a job as a garage attendant."

"Are you sure you want to stay in Leeds? You could come back home and work there and return to re-start next year? Or, if university really isn't working for you, you could get a job with some training towards a qualification of some sort?"

"No, I can sort this, Mum. I need to do it."Again, that confident reassurance.

I had to do something positive. "OK, but why don't we see if you can keep your hand in with studying a bit, part time, around your job?"

You seemed to think that was a reasonably good idea, so I tore round the university campus trying to find out how we could re-register you to re-sit the failed module, and perhaps continue with some other modules during the coming year, so that you did not lose the habit of studying or contact with your peer group on the course, and also could register some academic credits. But no-one would talk to me! You were an adult and so they needed your consent or involvement to offer any information, let alone advice. This came as a shock – at school parents' evenings the teachers had given detailed information on your progress and took note of what we said in response – it was a matter of shared concern and responsibility. Now, it seemed, little more than a year later, you were an autonomous adult, with sole responsibility for your own welfare, and we had no right to discuss your affairs with those in authority, even less influence them. So now – for the first time in your development we had a serious major issue to address, and nothing could be done – discussed even – without you being there or granting prior consent. Fortunately, I am pleased to say that since all this happened, in response to many more tragic university stories, the institutions have started to offer students, on their arrival, 'waiver' documents – enabling university staff to start discussions with parents should any worrying signs develop.

But for us, then, this was going to be a time-intensive process, more than I could devote around my full-time job, and so Dad, who worked part time from home, stepped into the breach. He spent the next three days with you in Leeds, organising meetings and visiting the various departments and tutors to chart out some meaningful study for you, around the core maths module, to keep you academically active in between your paid work. This arrangement continued for the rest of the academic year.

I continued to worry about your social situation as you were still detached from your peer group and it seemed that your current flatmates were formerly unknown to you, not friends encountered in the first year. I did not appreciate then that this tendency, again, was to be reinforced over the coming months and years, However, at our regular after-work suppers you assured me that you were back on track and doing fine, and I could only hope that this was true. Dad's view then was that you were lazy and lacking drive, but I felt that your unhappiness in Leeds had deeper roots than I had originally imagined, but roots which I could not understand. This was to be a constant difficulty for Dad and me – how to read and interpret the worrying events and unusual behaviour we were witnessing. Not only was it difficult to come to a view on what was going on, but we often reached a different view and ended up arguing over what to do about it. This was to become a regular source of friction between us, which, in turn, made us less inclined to talk about it at all.

The 21st April 2004 was approaching – your 21st birthday – and we asked how you would like to celebrate – would you like a party with your friends? "Just with the family" you said. So Dad, Matthew and I joined you for dinner in a trendy riverside restaurant on the fast-developing Leeds riverfront. With all four of us together for a number of hours I noticed you were decidedly less comfortable than when you and I shared our after work suppers. On the way back to Sheffield Dad remarked "He's not very sociable these days, and even decidedly peculiar sometimes."
"Yes, but I guess it can't be easy in his situation. His re-sit is coming up, and he will be feeling disappointed about losing the year, being separated from his peer group, and losing contact with his new friends. He'll also be worried about how it will be next term."
This response hid my own growing concern about your all-to-prickly disposition these days. Why did you always seem suspicious when we asked you innocent questions about your life, your work, anything? If I sensed you were anxious or unduly negative and asked you about it you were dismissive, suggesting that I was over-reacting. And when we engaged in 'small talk' at your birthday meal, you seemed to view us with disdain. Your whole demeanour looked shifty when engaging with waiters in restaurants, and what happened to that lovely smile of yours – it was rarely in evidence by now? You didn't help us to work out what was happening to you.

However, by early June, having discussed the content with Dad on several occasions before sitting it, you heard that you had passed your re-sit and assured us you were set to re-join the full course next term. I tried to persuade you to get a job in Sheffield for the summer (so that I could keep an eye on you) but you insisted on remaining with your work in Leeds. It seems so obvious, now, Alex. For whatever reason, you were not coping with life in Leeds. So I wanted you home, back in Sheffield where we could look after you again, make sure you were OK. But no – you were an adult now, and, feeling an adult, and I could understand why you did not want to capitulate and return to be 'looked after' by Dad and me.

While there, and Dad and I were away on holiday, you bought an old car with the money you had saved from your 21st. Dad was annoyed that you bought it off E-bay, without knowing anything about cars, and without seeking his advice – was this just another misguided effort to progress independently or bad decision-making as a result of a troubled mind? Questionable judgement again. Once more, Dad and I read this differently. I had started to think that something serious was behind it all, but Dad thought you were just becoming feckless, that you needed a 'kick up the backside'. And I wanted to protect you from his criticism for fear of it contributing to your anxiety. Nonetheless, I did feel better that you were at least going to be more mobile within Leeds and likely to travel back to Sheffield with greater frequency.

You had to change flats for the start of the next academic year, but you said you were looking forward to 'getting back into the course'. I felt better about you being in Leeds since your brother was to join you to start his music degree there, and you seemed pleased that he would be close at hand. Indeed, very quickly it turned out that you would regularly pick him up in your car to take him shopping; even better, you had started having 'jamming' sessions with him. Matthew would book a studio at the university and he would play keyboards or drums to accompany you on guitar. Now there were three of us eating out in Leeds about once a month, and it all seemed very companionable. Maybe things would turn out OK? This was a recurring problem over those first few years – my concerns would crystallise in response to a number of events or behavioural changes, only to dissipate when you seemed to return to your former confident, bouncy self. The apparent symptoms of some underlying condition were too vague and non-specific for us to be sure that there was indeed something to be worried about – and what it might be.

For instance, you were obviously feeling better about your course, and talking about possible future careers. I remember you coming in to my office one day.

"I've been thinking that I could become a social worker, as I may be better suited to a caring career than a commercial one in law or accountancy –what do you think?"

"Well, let's see what opportunities there are available at the moment", I said, as I brought up on the computer examples of the kinds of jobs that were currently being advertised in that sphere. "Why don't you visit the Careers Office and talk it through with them?" This felt a positive proactive train of thought and I was encouraged.

You did come home at weekends more regularly in your car, often to meet with old school-friends who were in town also, and I decided things were definitely improving – you had come through whatever had beset you the last two years. Perhaps you were a little quieter than usual at Christmas, but we let that pass. However, I knew you were still not completely comfortable with your life, as, when home for weekends, you would always repeatedly defer the time on Sunday evenings when you would leave us and set off up the motorway back to Leeds. Dad picked up on this "What's the matter with him? Why does he say he's going and then two hours later he's still hanging around, doing nothing in particular?" I had no logical answer.

An insight into how you were feeling at the time is evident from a letter you sent to Gran and which she gave to me several years later, shortly before she died. It confirms that you were aware that maybe you had not quite been yourself over Christmas, but maintained the usual positive stance on the future.

2 Station Parade
Kirkstall
Leeds LS5 3HG
February 2005

Dear Gran,

Sorry it took me a while to get in touch, but I've been quite busy. Thank you for the money you gave me at Christmas – I start to feel quite guilty with such generous relatives.

*I went up to Bury recently to take Dot (*my aunt who had not been able to join us the previous Christmas due to illness) *her Christmas presents with Matthew. She was pleased with the present you gave her – I can't remember exactly what it was, but have an image of a tablecloth? Now I write that down it sounds more like a shot in the dark than it did before. She said she would try and get in touch and was sorry she couldn't make it at Christmas time. She seemed bright, though, and treated me and Matthew to tea and biscuits and a belated slice of Christmas cake.*

I recently got my exam results and did quite well, although I was hoping for a little better. I felt a bit nervous in my exams, though, which I've never been burdened with in the past, and I knew it would have an adverse effect.

Sorry if I was a little distant or unwelcoming at Christmas, I've just been having a few troubles, which seem to permeate into family relations, but I'm completely over them now. They say youth is wasted on the youth, which in my interpretation is inevitable from the highpoint of experience and foresight, but youth is the time when you go through troubles and realise fully who you are, so you don't stumble on some mistakes perpetually. That's why I came to university, and that's exactly what's happened, but I realise I have been difficult and enigmatic, for which I apologise. University this term is exactly what I want it to be, and I'm really starting to enjoy my time here. Economics is closely similar to A level except more specific, thorough yet broad, accessible and applicable at the same time, which seems paradoxical – but it's difficult to explain. Philosophy has got a lot more complicated, and at first seems disconnected from reality, but encourages contemplation and logic, and its history is full of fascinating individuals.

*Recently my old friend came up to Leeds for a few days, as some French girls we met on holiday came up to Leeds. This was very surprising as I had not heard from them in a few years, but they were coming over for research with their university. It was quite difficult at first, and my slight knowledge of the French language didn't stand up too well, which always makes me feel like a stereotypical Europhobic Briton. It was a feeling akin to that when Sophia (*cousin in Luxembourg) *explained how many languages she was familiar with. Luckily, their English was even better than* *mine, and we had a good time. They were interested in English culture and – alas – we visited an art gallery. I have been to a few art galleries before, but seldom out of choice, yet it was quite enlightening. It is now on my 'to do list' to accustom myself with art and all its computations, but it isn't a high priority at present. We cooled down afterwards with a beer and a game of pool, which was closer to my area of expertise! It reminded me of going abroad, though, and – money permitting – I will go away to Europe this summer with a few friends.*

To help with money I recently got a delivery job with an Italian Pizza place, which has been an ambition since I saw Spiderman doing it in the recent film! I think Matthew is enjoying his course also, and more so since he immerses himself in music every hour of the day. I've started getting together with him in the music department at the university, to play together, which is a lot of fun. Whether it will go anywhere I'm not sure, but it's thoroughly enjoyable anyway. Thanks again for the money, which is very useful and enhanced my financial security. Hopefully I will go away in the summer and if I do I'll send you a top notch postcard! Are you going away this summer? I hope you are still enjoying your new flat and that all is going well.

Lots of love
Alex

You did get away that summer, Alex – but to Thailand with Ben. However, later I was to find out that your estimation in this letter of how you were faring must have been developed while wearing rose-tinted glasses.

.

Probably not long after you wrote that letter to Gran, in April 2005 we were in the Lake District for a walking weekend with our friends Sue and Alan. Over breakfast on Sunday morning, I took a call from you in which you explained that you had been mugged the night before in your flat in Leeds. The police had just left and you were not feeling too good. We arranged to meet you at the earliest opportunity in Leeds, and hurriedly packed up to set off down the motorway.

We met at Café Nero in Leeds city centre, and you looked amazingly relaxed under the circumstances – you always did like having a good street-based coffee while reading the paper – but it was clear you had been unnerved by the experience.

"The worst thing, Mum, is that my flatmates are blaming me, big-time, for the loss of their music equipment – because I'd gone out around midnight to get some cigarettes, and hadn't closed the door properly."

"What did the police say?"

"They said that a group of four young men had worked their way down the Kirkstall Road, trying to enter any premises that were less than secure, but they did not know their identities. I'd left the door on the latch mistakenly, so they came in and stole a load of musical equipment from the lounge next to my room, and then they are leaning over my bed, asking for cash. I only had about fifteen pounds, so they marched me off to the ATM to withdraw some more. When we got back to my room they thumped me and left."

We spent a couple of hours with you, and suggested that you come back to Sheffield for a short break, but you reassured us you would be fine and preferred to continue in Leeds. I was worried, though, because you would continue to have to deal with your housemates' ill-feeling – a suspicion that at a later date in discussion, you confirmed was true – a continuing source of difficulty with them. Didn't you already have sufficient difficulty with friendships, having lost contact with your university peer group, without giving this new set of potential friends reason to distrust you?

I was pleased, though, in the ensuing weeks, we had more regular phone contact. You were better at keeping your phone charged – and picking up! – than previously. And we shared, at a distance, a particularly remarkable Liverpool FC achievement – their winning the European Champions League after being 3-0 down at half-time. Dad and I were celebrating with champagne at the tennis club in Sheffield and gave you a ring.

"How great was that" Dad shouted into the phone.

"Yeah, amazing" could be heard, among a lot of noise your end. "It's been fantastic. I'm in the pub and the only real

Liverpool supporter, but everyone was cheering them on anyway. It's been a great night."

I responded, "We've been in contact with Sue and Alan and they are over the moon. They've had a houseful of LFC supporters with them, and were enjoying the post-match celebration. And I've just bought champagne all round at the club. Yes, it's very special. Speak to you soon Alex."

During that academic year we had regular conversations about your studies and your general well-being and you reassured us that things were well. It seems inconceivable now that we could have believed you, but around June time, having just started a holiday job in Leeds, you told us that you had passed your exams, but would have liked to have got better grades. We discussed individual grades in detail, and it all seemed very real, if a little disappointing all round. You reassured us that you could pull things round in the final year. When you returned from a holiday in Thailand with your old school-friend, Ben, again we took you back to a different flat in Leeds for the start of the new academic year in October 2005.

As usual, in the second week of term I arranged to meet you in town for tea after work, this time without Matthew, as he was busy. I arrived first, and as soon as I saw you walk into the restaurant I knew that you were not a student – you looked lovely, how good-looking you were – but your smart trousers and shirt belied the possibility that you had just come from a day of lectures or study. I said as much to you and heard that – yes, you had failed one of the exams again, and the re-sit in the summer, so were now working as a medical secretary at St. James' Hospital, pending taking another re-sit at the next opportunity. Devastation again. Take a deep breath. Try not to be judgmental and angry.

"Alex, it seems that university is not really good for you. Why don't you think about establishing yourself in work without a degree? You mentioned last year being interested in social work, and you can do that on day release from an entry-level job in a local council. You could come back to Sheffield to begin with, and work from home, while you sort out the kind of work you'd like long-term."

"No, Mum, I can do this. I'm not going to give up now."
"Is it the economics again? Can Dad help?"
"No, it's a philosophy module."
But I was at least as interested in knowing how you were getting on socially.
"Are you able to keep contact with your university friends, Alex?"
"Yes, I still see Paul and Caroline."
"Ah, Caroline – how is she getting on?"
"She's doing well, really enjoying her course."
"So do a crowd of you get together?"
"No, she and I go for a drink together quite often, just the two of us. We have to organise it each time in advance as her flat is across town at Clarence Dock."
"So, are you still just friends or is there more to it?"
"We're just friends – she has a boyfriend now. I'm really fond of her and wish I hadn't insisted we should be just friends ages ago, when she wanted it to be more."
I hadn't known of this before. "So why did you say that? If you've thought she wanted something more previously, though, Alex, it should be worth exploring this with her, surely?"
"Maybe. I'll think about it."

This was significant as it was the first time you had given us any indication that you had designs on a romantic relationship. In the last few years of school you were always out with 'the lads' – there were six of you in your group who would generally congregate at our house on a Friday night before venturing out on the town. We never saw you with a girl, and you never mentioned any liaisons with girls at all at home in Sheffield. The only such link was with Estelle in France. You and your school-friend Ben (whom we'd taken with us on your last holiday with us, to Spain) met Estelle and friends on the beach and spent a lot of time with them. It was clear she was fond of you as she kept in touch by e-mail and later Facebook, and this culminated in her and her friends arranging to meet you and Ben, in Leeds, a full three years later, on a college educational trip to the UK. Anyway, I swallowed my disappointment at this revelation and we had a pleasant meal together, of course.

But yet another miserable drive home to Sheffield down the motorway, pondering on your situation: three years at Leeds, with, as yet just the first year's exams in the bag; mostly isolated from any earlier friendship group; frustrated by having only a friendly rather than a romantic relationship with the first girl I had ever known you show an interest in. With your car, you had been coming back to Sheffield quite a bit at weekends, to see your friends who were still here. But it was clear from your reluctance to leave on Sunday nights – often only setting off as I was going to bed – that life in Leeds was not good. Dad showed increasing irritation on these occasions.

"We can't go on like this, Gill. He's all over the place, messing around – he's just taking the piss. He needs to knuckle down and get a proper job instead of thinking he can get a degree without trying hard. We should have let him get a loan instead of paying his fees, then he might have valued it more." Growing friction between us over this, but Dad only saw you at home – he didn't have the insight of my discussions with you, and observations of your behaviour, in Leeds.

"There's more to it than that. There's something seriously wrong. He's not just messing about, I think he may be depressed. He's not just unhappy, his personality seems to be changing."

"Depressed – huh! He just needs to pull his finger out."

Alex – we couldn't work out, or at least agree, on what was happening and what to do about it. The only language I had for how I found you, was that you were depressed – whatever that meant! But Dad could only ever conclude that you were 'messing around'. We were too ignorant to read what might be happening. Privately, I continued to think that you could be better off continuing in work, and establishing yourself in a job, rather than continuing at university. You had spoken quite positively about the experience so far, and perhaps the medical secretary job could be the basis for doing on-the-job training for something more inspiring in the NHS. I hoped that you might reach the same conclusion at some stage.

But it was not long before I had what I thought real evidence that you may be ill. For me this was a real turning point in my reading of the situation. You called into the office one afternoon for a chat, after taking the exam re-sit.

"It felt OK, so I think I should have passed it, Mum, so I'll be able to resume year three next October."

"That's great news, Alex, I hope you're right. Do you fancy going somewhere for tea – if you hang around for a short while I'll be ready to leave?"

"Thanks, but I need to go straight back to the flat as I agreed to go for a pint later with one of my flatmates." So you set off down the corridor from my office – but in the opposite direction from that of your flat.

"Alex – that's the wrong way to get back to the flat."

"I know – I'll go the long way round as I don't like walking across the open campus because everyone watches me and I feel uncomfortable."

"Don't be ridiculous, Alex, people have got more important things to do than to keep an eye on you walking across the grass!" But as the words came out, and I saw your reaction, I realised that you definitely had a problem – you were paranoid! This was a light-bulb moment. I realized that I could now talk to people – anyone who could help – about a potential condition that people could recognise and maybe respond to with positive advice

"Alex – sorry for the clever comment, but there really is something wrong if you feel that way – don't you think?"

"No, it's nothing Mum, it's just the way I feel at the moment."

"Well I think it would be worth seeing a doctor about these feelings, or at least going to the Student Welfare Office, just to check it out?"

"OK" you said, unconvincingly.

After you left I picked up the phone immediately and rang the number of my colleague Neil, the University's Director of Welfare. Fortunately, he was in the office, and I explained the situation and my concerns for you.

"Well, it certainly sounds like he needs help and advice, so he should make an appointment with us. If we think it necessary we can also suggest he make an appointment with a doctor."

"But I'm not sure he will do this – he didn't seem convinced of the need when he left me."

"OK, well I can agree with you now an appointment for him to see me personally, but if he doesn't turn up, I can't do anything about it – he needs to be willing to seek help." Here we go again – Alex is an adult, he is responsible for his own welfare, he is autonomous, it doesn't matter what you know or think...

We set a date for the following week, and I rang you to check that you could make it. You said you could and agreed to go. But of course you did not turn up. I arranged to have tea with you after work.

"Alex, why didn't you keep that appointment with Neil? His office's whole purpose is to deal with students' problems while they're here – you're not the only one."

"I just thought I'd feel stupid asking what to do over something so insignificant."

"But it's not insignificant, Alex, what about the ongoing difficulties in relation to your course? You never failed any exam while you were at school, and achieved higher A level grades than you needed for this degree course, so something is clearly wrong. Unless Dad's right, and you're just not trying hard enough?" Not surprisingly, this made you angry.

"Look I am trying, but it's just harder than I thought it was going to be – all right? I'll go and see a doctor about this, and see what they have to say, but stop going on."

Later in the week you said you'd seen a doctor, who had said apparently that there was nothing wrong with you, and you were wasting his time – but did you really go and see him? I was never quite sure – how could I be? You were an adult, of course, responsible for your own welfare... and so there was no way of checking. It was then that the full force of the boundaries to our understanding and influence became obvious. How would we ever get to find out what was going on, and get you to do something positive about it?

And then another issue was revealed one Saturday morning, with the following e-mail exchange between us.

29.01.2006
Alex
I tried to ring you on Saturday because Dad took a call from Lloyds Bank who wanted to speak with you about a 'personal finance' matter. Her name is Helen, on 0845-303222 – so please ring her on Monday. Is it because you're heavily overdrawn due to fixing the car? If so, do you want me to put some money into your account?
Had a lovely Saturday evening – Sue and Alan came for dinner as they were in Sheffield to see Will. They've just gone back, calling in at Manchester to see Alan's son and grandchildren.
Love Mum x

30.01.2006
You can put some money into my account if you want. Obviously I would be grateful, but can survive without it so you don't have to, and it won't change the situation if you do. Sounds like you had a good weekend.
Alex

By this time your emails could be quite terse to say the least – communication was continuing to decline – another symptom of your reluctance or inability to communicate adequately.

31.01.2006
When you say 'it won't change the situation even if you do' – surely there must be an amount that – if it is credited to your account– will negate the need, or at least reduce, the amount of interest you will need to pay? Please let me know how much is needed to make that difference. I can make a contribution instead of paying for the skiing trip that you don't want, and also chip in as an early birthday present – and if it's more than feels reasonable under those scenarios, I can make it an interest-free loan, with an open pay-back date for when you're back on your feet. You'll need to give me your account details for me to be able to transfer.
Mum.x

31.01.2006

Yes I agree. I am unsure as to what is a reasonable amount, but a few hundred would be very helpful. I know you must think I am being financially irresponsible but it is due to erratic decisions in the past (was this yet more questionable judgement – or just difficulty in coping financially as well as socially, Alex?) *Anyway I hope you are not forwarding this to dad, but I suppose that's your choice. If you want to transfer some money my account is 24069560, sort code 308760, with Lloyds TSB. Speak to you soon.*
Love Alex.

So now we could add to your difficulties of social interaction an inability to deal with finances. What were the 'erratic decisions in the past' I wondered? More issues about your judgement. However, I transferred the money, and told Dad that you'd just gone a little overdrawn paying to fix the car, and I'd helped you out. But when I next saw you, you were evasive on the issue and I never found out how much you were in debt or why. My sense of powerlessness to help you was growing as, though you seemed to be having problems on a wider range of fronts, you were clearly even less inclined to seek help or discuss them with me. You were also becoming at best unresponsive, at worst distant, to planning family activities. Dad and I had suggested we go on another family ski trip after Christmas, as we had all had a lovely time in Meribel in the previous New Year week, but you said you couldn't possibly spare the timeout from your studies. How could we argue with that?

Shortly after this there was a really upsetting incident, which was to constitute another 'first' in your apparent transformation, and, it seemed to me, a critical turning point. You and Matthew arrived home separately one Friday evening, unannounced, and you'd organised to meet your friend Richard J, who was also back in Sheffield for the weekend. It was a nice surprise to have you both home unexpectedly, so I offered to treat the three of you for a curry, while Dad was at the gym. You were all in high spirits and we were having a good time until I broached the subject of what you were all going to do after you left university. In a very light-hearted manner I said "Well, I think you all ought to have a clearer idea by now of how you are going to earn a living. Any ideas, Richard?"

"Not really, Gill, I,,,"

"Well one thing's for sure – none of us is hankering after the fucking lifestyle that you and Dad have" you spat out – loudly. I was absolutely stunned into silence, and could only stare at you blankly – it felt like a really hard slap across the face. Heads turned towards our table, Matthew looked even more stunned than I was and Richard J again started to say something.

"Alex, you can't ,,,

"I'm out of here!" And you got up and went outside, meal half eaten. Richard J followed. Mathew put his arm around me as tears welled up, but I went to the ladies to compose myself. This I managed, and when I returned, you were all eating your meals again, quietly.

"Sorry Mum – that was uncalled for" was all you could say. We finished our meals in subdued fashion and you and Richard J then went out for the night. Matthew was unable to fathom what had prompted such an outburst. You had never spoken to me like that before, and I logged another piece of evidence of personality change to heighten my level of anxiety. This was to be the beginning of several incidents revealing a new cold and angry streak to your character which had not been evident before, although, disconcertingly, it was alternated also with some interludes in which you seemed highly vulnerable, seeking advice and support more than you ever had previously. It seemed your personality had stretched itself as far as it could go in either direction – and I was uncomfortable seeing you at either of these extremes, the vulnerable or the angry.

An example of the vulnerable you. I remember not long after the curry outburst you ringing me up (unusual in itself, as I was always the one to ring you) and confiding that you'd been upset with some events at work, and were finding them hard to deal with. We chatted about these for a while, and I sympathised, while explaining that this kind of office politics seemed to be universal, an unavoidable feature of the workplace. You seemed consoled and then announced that you were really pleased with yourself in that you had managed to give up smoking – something Dad and I had been trying to persuade you to do for years. But the degree of significance you seemed to apply to this, and to other people's reactions to it, I did find perplexing – you seemed like a child seeking to please a range of adults and be suitably rewarded. Yet only a week or two later the other, angry, Alex revealed himself.

Dad and I had organised a holiday to South Africa for a month in April, and I took you out for a meal before we went, as we would be away for your birthday. You were fine then, but when I realised you had a suitcase we needed up in Leeds, and I asked if you could bring it into the office one day, you brusquely informed me that you would meet me at the university main entrance the following week. I saw your car approach and pull in to the lay-by, but you just opened the passenger door, pushed the case towards me, saying "Have a good time. I'll keep in touch as we agreed." Your face was emotionless, completely blank, and I felt the tears well up as the car pulled away. I can't begin to describe, Alex, how chilled I was, and I felt I shouldn't be leaving you for a month, not knowing how you would be when we returned. I always found it difficult to deal with the cold shoulder treatment. It seemed to deny the possibility of any affectionate tie between us.

At least you kept your pledge on maintaining communication – I usually received a curt response to my texts within thirty-six hours. But after a long drive along the south coast towards Cape Town, on the evening of 21st April, we rang you.
"HI Alex, happy birthday!!"
"Hm"
"What have you been up to today?"
"Not much"
"We're staying in the Birkenhead House hotel tonight and it's lovely, right on the water's edge. I thought we had to stay here when I saw it, having lived in Birkenhead for years. They have whale-watching from the terrace here in the winter."
"Hmm."
"Are you going out tonight? Doing anything to celebrate?"

"No, just going to watch TV."

"Can you not go out with Richard J or anybody?"

"No."

"OK, well happy birthday anyway, love, and we'll see you in about a week"

"Hmm."

"Bye then."

"Bye."

There seemed to be no connection between us at all. You had nothing to say, nothing to ask, and your voice was detached, disinterested, cold…

Surprisingly, you drove down to Sheffield the weekend of our return, and were perfectly pleasant. Yet a week later, we again experienced your darker side. We had planned another celebration – a meal for the four of us in Leeds at the beginning of May to celebrate Matthew's 21st. I had arranged we would all meet at a new restaurant, again on the waterfront in Leeds after work. Dad drove up from Sheffield and was the last to arrive. We had a very enjoyable meal, talking about the holiday, showing some photos, with Matthew opening his cards and presents afterwards. Just as coffee was served, Dad opened up a conversation about how he thought some friends of ours were making some serious mistakes about how they were bringing up their son, as he seemed to be becoming spoilt.

"Anyone would think we were experts at bringing up children", I responded – a light-hearted riposte to possible smugness on Dad's part, I thought.

"Yes, I know how fucking rubbish you think I've turned out, Mum, but there's no need to rub it in!", as you jumped up from the table and stormed off to the toilet. Fortunately there were few people left in the restaurant at this stage to hear your outburst.

"What was all that about?" queried Dad, completely taken aback. I explained what had happened months earlier at the curry house in Sheffield.

"Can you explain that outburst, Matthew?" I asked him again.

"No, but I'll try and find out what's happening later." He and you had arranged to go to a club after the meal. Again we had a subdued few minutes while we paid the bill, and soon we were dropping you two off at the club venue.

That was the first time Dad had really witnessed and been surprised by your unusual behaviour, and during our drive back home down the M1 I felt that he was maybe now closer to my way of thinking that you weren't just suffering from a lack of drive and application.

After this incident you came home for the weekend a couple of weeks later – it was Spring Bank Holiday. Matthew had not been able to determine a sensible reason for your outburst, and neither Dad nor I felt able to make reference to it. On the Friday evening the three of us had an enjoyable few drinks in the pub over the road, and we didn't want to 'rock the boat'. Dad and I had both started to adopt a wariness to our dealing with you by now – we knew we had to be careful, and also expect – and deal sensitively with – negative and difficult responses.

On Saturday morning you asked Dad to have a look at the car with you as the engine had not been firing properly recently. One minute I could see the two of you leaning over the bonnet and the next you were clearly having an argument, with Dad gesticulating wildly and marching in towards the house. "Bloody idiot. What's the matter with him?"

You came trailing after him, "Sorry Dad."

"What's the matter?" I interjected.

"That boy needs to sort himself out – he's not fit to own a car. The engine was virtually seized up and he couldn't remember when he'd last put any oil in it. And I can't believe he's putting anywhere near enough effort into his course. We should have made him take out a loan rather than paying for him."

"OK, calm down, let's not over-react", and as I said it a horn sounded in the front drive, and there was your friend Andy's car in the drive.

"I'm off out of here", you shouted, and you were gone.

Dad and I had had these kinds of conversations several times by now and I responded in the usual vein.

"I keep telling you he's not right. He's not happy in Leeds, but it's more than that, he's troubled. I think he may have depression, but I don't know if he's seen a doctor yet."
"Depression? Is that what you call it? I call it taking the piss. He just needs to get a grip, he's completely feckless."
"As I keep saying, you don't see what he's like in Leeds when we go for a meal after work these days. He gets all twitchy and agitated, and doesn't relate to the waiters properly – he can't look them in the eye. I think he's paranoid."
"Oh yes, sure, let's feel really sorry for him shall we?" he said, and then he too disappeared off to the study.
At that moment I understood perfectly both your points of view in this exchange, but how could I get each of you to understand the other? I could not find the answer to this, and I didn't feel able to explore the issue further with Dad, rather preferring to let him calm down so we could all start again later in the weekend. The strain on our relationship was growing, each of us with different views on what was happening to you, and I knew it would probably be a continuing source of conflict in future.

A couple of hours later, your friend Andy dropped you back at home, and you seemed in better spirits, so I suggested a walk to Forge Dam as it was a lovely warm sunny day. You seemed to have resumed your good humour and readily agreed. I would have liked to have enjoyed that walk as mother and son ought to be able to, speaking casually about mutual interests and concerns, while enjoying the sun on our backs and the light flickering through the trees on a Bank Holiday weekend afternoon. But I felt I had to pin you down on where you were at – mentally, emotionally, socially. And you were surprisingly open to this discussion, perhaps more relaxed away from Dad's disapproving glances, and finding it easier to talk in the neutral territory of Whitely Woods..
"We're really worried about you, Alex – you don't seem to be very well organised in general, so how are your studies going?"
"Well, the philosophy is fascinating, and I'm really enjoying it. I like most of the economics too, although the mathematical elements are a bit tedious."

"If you have any more difficulties with that, you will discuss it with Dad, won't you?"

"Yes, of course, but it's not necessary at the moment."

"OK, so are you up to date with all your essays then?

"Yes, I'm working on one to hand in next week and I'll easily finish it on time.

We sat in the sun by the dam, drinking coffee and watching the walkers go by. The Bank Holiday had brought out many families with children who were excitably feeding the ducks. A young couple with a baby in a buggy walked past our bench.

"I do need to be more responsible, I know that, Mum."

"Yes indeed, but what made you say that?"

You laughed and pointed to the couple "Well, look at them. They're about my age with a baby, and I can't even organise just my own life!"

I smiled, pleased at your apparent self-awareness, after so many recent displays of bad judgement. But walking back along the path, with the sun warming my back, I felt really close to you, and full of hope – optimism even – that you would be able to deal successfully with whatever it was that was troubling you, and manage to get your life back into shape. All either of us could do was to discuss how things were going well in your job at St. James' and consider that maybe when you went back to complete your degree next year, perhaps you should opt for something in the public service arena rather than the commercial sector, as we had discussed before. When we got home, at my suggestion, you set things right with Dad, assuring him you were going to be more organised, before leaving for Leeds, waving us both goodbye.

But yet again this was your misguided reassurance. The following Wednesday, 31st May 2006, was to herald the trigger for a new and anguish-laden phase in the life of the whole Holt household. Life was never going to be the same again.

4.   The Breakdown – 31st May 2006

When I arrived home from work that evening to find your car
once again in the drive, I was immediately apprehensive as
to what this might signify. The plan, as always on a
Wednesday, was for a quick change of clothes for my
weekly tennis match at 7pm. I walked into the kitchen to find
a huge pile of your belongings in the middle of the floor, and
you sitting in the conservatory, gazing out of the window. It
only took one glance to register that all was not well. You
looked decidedly uncomfortable in your black anorak with
the zip pulled tight up unnaturally under your chin. "What's
the matter, Alex?" You didn't answer, but just shook your
head and grimaced. I went through to the study to ask Dad.
"What happened, what has he said?"
"Nothing much. I can't get any sense out of him. The first I
knew was I picked up a message from him on my phone
after leaving the dentist earlier, saying that he couldn't cope
any more so he was coming home to Sheffield. He arrived
about an hour ago, and doesn't seem to be able to explain. I
don't know what's the matter with him, don't know what to
say or anything."

I made a phone call to give my apologies for tennis and
returned to the conservatory. "Alex, what made you come
home? What's wrong?"
"I couldn't stay in Leeds, Mum, I had to come home."
"OK, love, but what is the matter? You seemed so calm and
settled about what you needed to do last weekend."
"I know, but I don't often feel that good, particularly in Leeds.
You don't realise there are terrible people in Leeds, Mum.
There are druggies and they are coming after me – they're
trying to kill me. Even my flatmates – they come into my
room when I'm not there."
At this, you looked quite desperate, your eyes widely staring,
and you were tugging at the zip on your cagoule, zipping the
collar right up over your chin. I gave you a big hug, and then
we both sat down again.
"Why do you think they would do that, Alex? What are they
after? Don't you think you may be imagining it?"

"No, you don't realise, there are lots of drug dealers in Leeds, and they want to kill me. I'm worried they will follow me here. And my flatmates are spies – they go into my room when I'm not there and take things."

"But when you moved in, you said they were really friendly and you got along well."

"Yes, but it didn't last. And now the druggies have followed me to Sheffield, I can hear them"

"Alex, I really don't think that's likely. Can you hear them now?"

"No, but I did earlier."

"I think your mind may be playing tricks on you, love. Remember you were going to see the doctor in Leeds about the paranoid thoughts you were having months ago? We discussed it a few times. Did you go?"

"I told you, Mum, I went – in fact I went twice – and they told me not to waste their time."

I wasn't sure whether or not to believe this, and to this day I still don't know if you did.

"OK, well, we'll go to our doctors' tomorrow and see what they have to say, shall we?"

"OK Mum but they'll be just the same, I bet."

"Right, well let's have some tea now, and then we can talk a bit more."

I went back to the study to speak to Dad.

"OK, he's agreed to go to the doctor tomorrow morning. We could both go, but I'm hosting a big meeting tomorrow, and cancelling would cause problems, so are you all right to go with him, and I'll come back after the meeting?"

"Yes, that's fine"

"I won't leave for work, though, until we have an appointment"

Back in the kitchen, Alex was hovering around, still in his anorak.

"Why don't you take your anorak off Alex – are you cold?"

"I feel safer in this."

For a couple of hours that evening I tried to get to the bottom of how you were feeling and what was wrong. You were more open than you had been for months about how you felt, but I couldn't relate to what you were saying. In the end you seemed more comfortable, and we chatted in a relaxed manner about more normal topics. Having received your reassurance that you would go with one of us to the doctor tomorrow, I bid you goodnight.

"OK, love, I need to get ready for bed now, maybe you should too?"

"No, I'm not tired yet. I'll read for a bit."

You then turned to me and, with the softest eyes I had seen in you for a long while, said "Don't ever change, Mum."

"What do you mean?" I smiled.

"You're so innocent" I wasn't sure what to make of this, particularly after so many hostile and antagonistic incidents in recent months, but took it as a compliment and hugged you.

"Yes, well never forget how much I love you – how much Dad and I both love you. We'll get you some help tomorrow. Night night."

"Night."

Dad had been hovering in and out of the kitchen all evening trying to pick up on what was going on, and he would keep an eye on you after I went up to bed.

1st June

I came downstairs at 7.30 am to find you, once again, sitting in the conservatory, still in your anorak, scribbling on an A4 pad, clearly into about your fifth or sixth page. "Have you been sitting here all night? What are you writing?" You obviously didn't want me to know what it was as you shuffled the papers together and pushed them away saying "I'm hungry, let's have some breakfast." While you were eating, Dad came down and gestured for me to talk with him. He told me that half an hour after I'd gone to bed the night before, from the study he heard you shout "Mum" at the top of your voice as you ran into the hall. He had come and held you, asking what was wrong and you had said "They've come to get me, can't you hear them?" Dad had said he could hear nothing, everything was OK, but you insisted that their voices were clearly audible just outside the study window.

After a hasty breakfast, I made the appointment with the doctor, gave you a hug, and told you to be as open as possible with him, and agreed with Dad that he would ring me at the office with the outcome. Driving up to Leeds I prayed that at last you might get some professional help to identify the reason for your troubles and help you deal with them.

When I rang home later Dad was upbeat. Initially he had been worried that you might get dismissed from the appointment with no diagnosis, since to every question posed by Doctor Childs you made a sensible and articulate response – giving every impression of a content and well-adjusted young man. This we came to realise was a particularly fickle aspect of your 'condition' – how quickly you could flip into and out of a troubled state. But towards the end of your allotted time, Dad recognised the moment when Dr Childs' countenance at last registered an issue. In answer to his question as to whether there was anything you were feeling really good about, you replied that you were proud of having given up smoking recently and that it was good to see so many people passing you in their cars clearly showing their admiration for your achievement. At this stage he said he would organise a visit from the Early Intervention Team, who would visit the house later that morning to make a more thorough assessment. By the time I rang Dad, they had just left our house, having spent an hour with you, and you had explained that you felt much better than the previous evening. They told Dad that they would make an appointment for the next day with their psychiatrist, who would be able to make a full diagnosis.
"Will he come to the house?" I said, thinking it might be difficult to get you out to an appointment again. "Yes" Dad replied, "and Alex has seemed fairly calm since they've gone, listening to music in his room. I've been up a few times and he seems fine."
"OK, I'll be leaving shortly. See you later." Little did I expect what a terrible revelation would be waiting for me back in Sheffield.

I almost felt hopeful, that though the situation had now reached crisis proportions, it could hence be dealt with – faced up to and dealt with. We could get a diagnosis and appropriate treatment. The professionals would explain to us what was wrong and how they and we could help you deal with it. You would be back home with us in Sheffield and we could repair any damage to family relationships, working together towards your recovery and getting your life back on track.

Approaching the drive I mused about how you might have spent the afternoon, perhaps confiding some of your deep troubles, at last, to your father. I imagined the coming weeks, in which, with time out, you and he could bond again through shared outdoor exploits in the summer sunshine; that through cycle rides into the Peaks or jointly tackled projects in the garden, you could find more pleasure again in each other's company – and you would come through this, whatever 'it' was.

Unnerving, then, to enter the hall and find an eerie silence; thoughts of you both even then enjoying some pursuit elsewhere were quickly rendered unlikely. The burglar alarm had not been activated, so someone was in the house. And I wondered why the visit this afternoon from the Early Intervention Team, precipitated by Doctor Childs should have left a distinctively hospital smell in the air, as I climbed the stairs to your room. But the smell was something more specific, much worse...

At the top of the stairs, outside the bathroom was your CD player, with my double Stevie Wonder CD cover, both daubed in blood. I turned a corner on the landing, and there was the horror of it all – my beautiful son sat cross-legged amongst puddles of congealing blood, a riot of red streaks on every surface creating a veritable war zone of the neatly tiled bathroom. Your face was wan, your eyes were dim, and an icy shard slid through my heart as a loud cry emerged from my throat.

Rising panic constrained my legs as they took the stairs two at a time to reach the phone downstairs – every second was going to count. Dad had arrived back in the house after posting a letter and was striding upwards past me on the stairs, having heard my shout, groaning – incredulous that this could be happening. My first emergency services call – how could the receptionist be so calm and unaffected? Why couldn't she tell me when the ambulance would arrive? How could I know, when she asked, how long you had been in this state?

Back upstairs now, and Dad was on the bedroom floor with you on his lap, holding towels tightly round your arms and slapping you hard.
"When's your birthday? What day is it today? Don't close your eyes" – desperate attempts to keep the door from finally closing. You were cold to touch and looking paler. "Is he still conscious?" from the emergency services receptionist.
"Only just – when will the ambulance be here?" I shrieked, running down the stairs to have the door open ready for when they arrive – why aren't they here yet? Looking frantically in each direction from the gateway, and then I hear it – nee-naa-nee-naa-nee-naa. Thank God.

After the initial assessment at the Northern General an A and E nurse came to tell us they were taking you up to surgery and we could accompany you upstairs to theatre. As they pushed you out of the lift your eyes opened and you looked up at Dad.
"Do you think I'll ever be able to play guitar again, Dad, when my wrists are such a mess?"
"I'm sure they'll be able to sort it, Alex" said Dad, turning away so you would not see the tears welling.
But this seemed to be a good sign – you were thinking of life after this.

How I prayed, in that tired-looking waiting room in the Northern General, not far from where the plastic surgeon was exploring the extent of the damage you had wrought and putting you back together. It took him nearly four hours – how long did it take you to inflict the damage, Alex? Dad, fearing the worst and weeping uncontrollably, was saying "now he's done it once it will be easier to do it again."

You were pale and motionless, among the tubes and bandages in the hospital bed, blood coursing back into your veins, but no light yet in your eyes, my heart was heavy but hopeful. Whatever it takes, I said to myself, I will make sure that you not just find a reason to live but also to enjoy a positively fulfilling life. But you must help me Alex.

"You need to be strong for him when you come back tomorrow" said the nurse. "He'll be feeling bad from the physical effects of his injuries and the operation, but also suffering emotionally and psychologically from failing in his attempt, and knowing the affect it will have had on you." We encouraged each other on the way home that we would be able to do this, but could not then imagine the new and bewildering – sometimes terrifying – world you, and we, were about to enter.

After a few hours' sleep, I awoke with a start on 2 June, instantly recalling the devastating events of the previous evening, and with an overriding need to 'get busy' – to start to address the issue, to get people on your case, to find reasons for you to want to go on living. The hospital had told us we could visit you any time after 10am, so we had a couple of hours to get going. My thoughts went immediately to Caroline. She was the one person outside the family whom I knew you really cared about, and that she regarded you – at least – as a good friend. Perhaps a visit from her would lift your spirits? But how could I get in touch with her? I didn't have any contact details, didn't even know her surname. All I knew was that she was studying Biochemistry at Leeds and was in her final year. Immediately I was on the phone to my work colleague the Student Welfare Director at Leeds University.
"Neil – I need your help. We got Alex to a doctor yesterday, he was seen by the community team, but later slit his wrists and the hospital just managed to save him."
"Oh Gill, I'm so sorry. That's dreadful. But how can I help?"
"Well, I thought it would help if he could see a close friend of his from Leeds – Caroline – they've been friends for the whole time in Leeds. But I don't know how to contact her, and thought you could find some details on the University system – she is in her final year of Biochemistry, and there shouldn't be more than one Caroline?
Any other time, of course, I would have known that this was not going to lead anywhere – I would have known that such

information could not be located and shared in such a way –
but I was desperate.

"Gill I'm sorry, but that is not possible – you know all about
data protection. No-one here, not just me, can divulge any
such details to you."

"Yes, but this is a life and death situation, Neil, surely
different rules can apply then?"

"No, they don't. But I really think that this might not be a
good idea anyway, from Alex's point of view. Given what he
has just done, how he must feel right now, and bearing in
mind he has not wished to open up about his condition to
anyone up to now, do you really think he would like his friend
to visit him like this 'out of the blue'?"

"OK, I see what you mean. Thanks anyway Neil."

"Take care, Gill, and give me ring if I can help in any other
way."

I wasn't convinced, however – even if you would be shocked
to see her, maybe she would be able to persuade you out of
these dark thoughts. Dad arrived downstairs looking
dreadful.

"Who was that?"

"I had a thought that Alex's friend Caroline might be the best
person to see him and persuade him that he did have a
reason to live, but I don't have any contact details, don't
even know her surname. I thought Neil from the university's
welfare office could find out for me, but he's not allowed to."

"His phone's in the living room – I'll have a look – he's
probably got her number stored."

Sure enough, it was there, and we now had her number. So
I took a big breath and rang it. It went into voicemail. "Hello
Caroline. This is Gill, Alex's mum. I hope you don't mind me
ringing but Alex has been taken really ill. He's in hospital,
and I wondered if you might be able to visit him? He's very
fond of you and I'm sure seeing you would help lift his spirits.
Anyway, do give me a ring if it's possible. Thanks. " Within
half an hour she rang back, saying she was now at her
parents' home in Glossop and would be happy to come and
visit you – I said you'd had a 'breakdown' and we agreed
that Dad or I would come and pick her up to bring her over
the next day.

On arrival back at the hospital we both found it difficult to live up to the requirement to be brave and positive when we saw you: sitting up in bed and looking physically fine, but with really bulky padding around both your wrists and lower arms, and completely blank eyes, seemingly devoid of any emotion. It was clear from the stares by other older patients on the ward that all had worked out why you had been hospitalised and were wondering what could have led you to such action. We had been told that the staff were waiting for a visit from a psychiatrist who would assess your mental condition to decide what happened next. It was not easy to communicate with you but one thing you were clearly determined about was that no-one you knew should know what you'd done. You definitely didn't want to talk about what had prompted you to take your own life, and demanded that we should take you home immediately as you were fine.

The psychiatrist and a nurse arrived shortly after us, so we left them with you for the assessment. They came out to see us to explain that they had told you that you needed to spend some time in a mental health ward where they could determine the best treatment for your condition and prescribe appropriate medication to manage your symptoms. You had agreed to do this voluntarily, otherwise they would have 'sectioned' you – invoked a power under the Mental Health Acts – to enforce your hospitalisation. We would need to wait till the following day for the ward – fortunately, it seemed, in a small community mental hospital not far from where we lived –to arrange for a bed to be available, when they would send a taxi to pick you up. They said it was fine for me to travel with you and see you settled in to the local hospital.

I managed to remain reasonably composed as I escorted you out of the hospital, Alex. You were completely uncommunicative and still looked completely blank; walking slightly ahead of me with the mental health nurse from the local hospital, while the ward nurse who had been charged with accompanying us to the taxi was clearly uncomfortable. "What a good-looking lad he his. I'm sure you'll sort things out with him." I looked again sideways at you, as we caught you up, and thought, "Yes, I know he is. What is it that could have brought my good-looking, bright and sensitive boy to this pass?" I remembered my optimism of the previous days – that you were now in the care of professionals: people who would understand your condition, when we were completely bewildered; people who would know what to do to make you better, and advise us on how to help. Yet these people had not detected your suicidal tendencies, the depth of your despair. In time, they, as did we, would come to realise how adept you were at disguising your true state of mind.

5. Early Intervention – June 2006 to 2007

I can't begin to describe how bewildered, how helpless, I felt as we drove across Sheffield in silence. Why were you so disturbed? How could we not have known? How could we help you recover? And what was a mental health ward like? The Michael Carlisle Centre was a modern mental health annex built next to a larger Victorian-era hospital that had been demolished some years ago. As such, it was a small two-storey building, a bleak concrete structure built in the early sixties, and not in good condition. However, it was quite small and so the scale felt more human and personal than the Northern General we had just left. But no-one had prepared me – and no doubt you – for our arrival into Chester Ward, where you were to be admitted.

The nurse rang the bell at the ward entrance – the door was locked. We were let in and hovered in a corridor while the staff member went off to find the senior nurse who was to supervise your admission. He came down the corridor, introducing himself: "Hello, I'm Josh, the senior nurse in charge, and you must be Alex?" and turning to me, "And you must be Mum? Do you wish to stay with Alex while he is admitted?"
"Err, yes please," I said, puzzled. Surely that was obvious? Oh, I forgot, you were an autonomous adult...........
"OK Mrs Holt, please could you wait here while I just have a few words with Alex to see if he is happy to have you present. Alex, could you come in here please?"
You disappeared into a little room, leaving me in the corridor wondering how anyone could think I would not wish to stay around and be involved. I looked around, taking in the general environment, and was aware immediately of several people of varying ages wandering about without much apparent purpose. One was dressed in pyjamas, another was talking to himself. It came to me that the only knowledge (if that's what it was) of the inside of a mental health ward was its depiction in 'One Flew Over the Cuckoo's Nest', a film I had watched about thirty years ago. I remembered that it was based in America, and hoped that this one would not be so distressing.

Two minutes later I was invited to join you and Josh, and sat down in the interview room. It felt strange talking about what was to happen in that tiny little room with three easy chairs crowded into the spaces left over around small piles of children's play equipment – why on earth should all that be there? – But I didn't ask. Josh explained that you had given your permission for me to be involved in the discussion about your treatment, and I thought, "Well, thanks a lot. We've just managed to save our son from dying, waited through an agonising night while he was stitched together again, and I might not have been able even to hear what would happen next!"

This had been, and would continue to be, a recurrent theme in our dealings with anyone in 'the system'. No-one would discuss any details about your situation with us unless they had your explicit consent – you were an autonomous adult and we no longer had jurisdiction over you. Up until now this had been no more than a serious irritant in our attempts to intervene in your affairs to support you. But from now on it seemed that the 'Early Intervention Team' of mental health nurses and social workers – the ones whom you'd first encountered with Dad the other day – would have greater rights than we in this matter, even though they had not realised how serious was your frame of mind, and it was we who found you and got you to hospital before it was too late. This is not a criticism of 'the system', rather an obvious reflection that as your parents we had a far greater motivation to be vigilant in keeping you safe, and – in this case – greater opportunity to do so, since it was to the family home you (not unnaturally) chose to return to in this time of crisis.

Josh then went on to ask you all sorts of administrative questions about your personal details, and then asked what had brought you to take the action you did. I could tell that you were only engaging because you had to, and the description you gave of your experience of paranoia and voices was fairly thin. I added additional detail of the conversations we had had recently, particularly the night you arrived home from Leeds, and Josh asked you if you still had suicidal thoughts. You said you didn't but I'm not sure either of us believed you. He then explained that you would probably stay with them for a few weeks while they sorted out your treatment and medication and kept you under observation. After that you would be allowed home, with regular appointments with the Early Intervention Team for ongoing supervision and support. Josh said I could bring in from home things you would need, and you asked that I bring in your phone and a couple of books you would like, but he said that to begin with you would not be permitted your phone as you would need a 'low level sensory environment', and that we could communicate with you if necessary through the ward office. I asked you if I could inform your two Sheffield-based friends where you were so they could visit you, and you agreed, provided that I didn't tell them the full details of what had happened.

So that was it. Our son was now in a mental health ward and the three of us started a bewildering journey: for you this would involve further distressing developments in your symptoms which would reinforce your suicidal tendencies in future, regular hospitalisation, and the vagaries of so-called community care; for Dad and I, unimagined anguish in watching the apparent 'melt-down' of our son while trying to provide the most support and care we could in the face of our ignorance of both your condition and the confusing mental health world.

Driving back from the hospital with Dad, I realised that Neil from the university had been right – you would not thank me for bringing Caroline over to see you in your current condition in hospital. As soon as I got home I rang her and explained that maybe you would not wish her to see you so soon, and she was fine about it. Telling the family what had happened was difficult to say the least. This was mainly down to Dad as I had only my sister in New Zealand and Auntie Dot in Manchester, both of whom I thought could be spared the worst. I told them you were in hospital having had a 'breakdown', and was grateful that my parents did not live to have to deal with this blow. Gran was devastated and totally bewildered by the real news, and Dad was in tears talking to her on the phone. "But they will be able to make him better, won't they, Andrew?"she asked. We didn't know the answer to that one.

The morning after our nightmare I had sent an email to the office explaining that you were seriously ill in hospital and that I would need a few days' leave. They were very concerned and supportive, and told me to take as much as I needed. A former close colleague from Leeds City Council who was told this when trying to contact me a few days later, rang from work. I told her the full details and she was completely silent for a minute or so – the news was too big and distressing to process quickly. We regularly met socially after work and she was acutely aware of my growing concerns about you – but suicide? The reaction from the few close friends I chose to reveal the full facts to was the same. To most of our friends, you had 'had a breakdown' – that just seemed easier all round. And anyway, at that stage, we had nothing more specific to say. There had been no diagnosis.

A few days later, once you were less volatile having come to terms with your situation, we had a meeting with you and the psychiatrist, in which he explained that you had clearly been having serious psychotic episodes for some time that had been building up and getting worse. Sometimes, he said, these could be triggered by taking drugs but you had been tested for this at the Northern General, with negative results, and had yourself denied taking any. I remembered, then, what you had said on the night of your return to Sheffield about 'the druggies' in Leeds who were 'out to kill you', and made a mental note to ask you later if you had taken any drugs while in Leeds. So you were now on a course of anti-psychotic medication, which would take a week or so to kick in and may need some adjustment over time, and they would keep you in hospital until they saw positive results, after which you could be discharged. Once you were home, the Early Intervention Team would be available to help Dad and I support you in your 'recovery'.

You were reasonably calm and this was a fairly reassuring meeting, but during that first week or so in Chester Ward, when taking it in turns to visit you each day, Dad and I were shocked by what we saw and experienced there: sometimes

approaching your room in the first few days and hearing you howl in despair; steeling ourselves to absorb your angry provoking language in challenging our 'allowing' you to be there; seeing 'lost souls' wandering around the ward sometimes seeking to engage us in seemingly pointless conversations; observing the huddle of individuals who congregated with you in the garden near the front entrance for their hourly smoke, surrounded by a sea of fag-ends. Matthew found visits equally difficult to begin with. You were pleased that both your friends – Richard J and Richard G – had visited you but I still do not know at this stage whether you told them the whole truth of how you arrived there.
.

After a while we became more accustomed to the experience, and you less angry at your surroundings, and after a couple of weeks, you were able to spend increasing time with us for each of five or six days outside the ward, until you were discharged. But it was clear even then how self-conscious you were destined to be about your condition and experience. Do you remember that first walk we went on one lovely Sunday at the end of June? You asked if we could go out to the Peak District and we went to Castleton, where we had a short walk and then a pub lunch. Walking down the main street in Castleton, I was surprised to see you put on your sweatshirt, as it was extremely hot. But then I realised – you were pulling down on the sleeves to cover the savage scars evident on your wrists.

You'd already been told you would be discharged from hospital the next day, and, enjoying the sunshine in the beer garden, we had our first discussion about your future.
"I'll get a job in Sheffield till term starts again", you said, and I was pleased that for the first time since you went to Leeds, you would be with us through the summer.
"Yes – they may even need people in the Hallamshire or Northern General, and you would have a good chance of getting a job there", I replied.
"I don't see why, when I left the job at St. James' so suddenly."
"Yes, but they obviously thought a lot about you there", I explained.
"How do you know that?"

"When I contacted the agency (I had found your worksheet from the recruitment agency among your things) to explain your sudden absence from work, they expressed their sympathy that you were seriously ill in hospital, and said that your line manager at St. James' spoke very highly of you – she had said you were a good and reliable worker with a pleasant manner, who would turn yourself to anything asked of you." You smiled at this, saying "Well it was often really boring actually, so I was always looking for something different to do", and I continued "Which actually is much the same response that you had from your first real job at John Lewis. I remember you telling me what your boss had said on your last day – apart from ragging you about how they thought you looked like Elvis!; also that when you got back from Australia, your former colleagues from the lighting department arranged to meet with you after work as they enjoyed your company."

This produced another half-smile, so I was emboldened to continue "I've been thinking that maybe continuing in work for a while, till you feel more recovered from all this anxiety, could be the best way forward, rather than returning to Leeds in October."
"No, Mum, I need to finish my course – only one more year – I can do that."
"But it seems to me that living there with random flatmates again is not going to help you recover your confidence – better to have some structure to your days with work, and living back with us for a while? The University will allow you to defer completing your course under the circumstances"
"No, I'm definitely going to complete the course straight away. I can do it."
At that point I backed off, thinking that there would be other opportunities to persuade you otherwise between now and October.

I had been right about the job prospects at the hospitals. On your first day after discharge you found a couple of possible jobs advertised on their website and sent in your applications. Two weeks later you had had a successful interview and would be starting at the Northern General the following Monday. It is six or seven miles from our house, and would require two buses, into and out of town, so you chose to use Dad's bike instead, and I remember feeling really good about the whole situation – healthy bike rides, a solid job and living under our roof, where we could make you feel safe and supported. I felt we had every chance of getting you back on track with your life.

Your job did go well, and you seemed to be comfortable in this situation, if very resistant to the idea that you should take medication on an ongoing basis. "I'm fine now. I don't need these tablets anymore."
"Alex, we've been through this many times with Sarah", I replied.
Over recent weeks, while building up time with us out of hospital, we had had regular meetings at home with the Early Intervention Team. Sarah was your allocated Community Mental Health (CMH) nurse, and she had spent three or four hours with the three of us, helping us to understand what they knew of psychosis, how the medication helped, but how you had to keep it going continuously, and not stop once you started to feel better. It was clear from these discussions that this could be a problem for the future.

At these sessions, in private discussions not involving you, we quizzed Sarah and her colleague psychologist on the prospects for your recovery from this, and how long it might take for you to get back to normal. After all, this is what you also asked of clinicians in relation to illnesses, wasn't it? But it was immediately very clear that they had no idea at all about your prognosis.
"With psychosis, it tends to be something that develops in late teens or early twenties, and can be triggered by drugs or some personal trauma. But it can develop without any stimulation, and the degree to which it is treatable, by drugs or other therapies, is highly variable", Sarah explained.
"Some people with this condition can be clear of symptoms after a period of medication, and others appear to 'grow out of it', but others are never quite clear of the condition, and have to learn to manage it", added the psychologist. "It is not possible at this stage to tell which category Alex is in."
Great – nobody had a clue what would happen from here!

This ongoing uncertainty, the lack of a clear path to recovery, was to be a particularly grievous aspect of your illness, By now I had started reading up on mental illness – its causes, treatments etc – wishing to be better informed about what to expect and how to help. I had come across various campaigning organisations who wrote about how little investment went into research on mental illness when compared with the vast resources ploughed into the 'big three' physical illnesses – cancer, diabetes and heart disease – a claim I was able to verify from my knowledge of the relative proportions spent in these areas in Leeds University. It was not surprising, therefore, that better and earlier diagnosis, and progress on developing effective medication and therapies, had been historically rather slow in relation to mental illness, which certainly seemed to be the 'poor relation' in the NHS system.

While Sarah agreed with Dad and me that a job in Sheffield would be preferable to rushing back to Leeds, you were increasingly adamant that you would not delay finishing the course. This meant that you would be outside her jurisdiction for support – and out of our ambit of direct involvement. We asked if you could continue to get the necessary medication and she explained that this was not possible without ongoing supervision from a clinical professional, and you would need to register for this in Leeds. We asked if she could set that up, but apparently it was not possible – again, only you could do this. The equivalent team in Leeds was called Aspire, and you would need an assessment meeting with them to secure appropriate support.
"Well I'm not going through all that again – I'm OK now, anyway, I don't need medication anymore" you couldn't get out quick enough.
"But we've discussed this before, Alex, – you need to continue the medication to continue feeling better" Sarah volunteered. "I can give you contact details for them."
"That's a great idea, thank you, Sarah", I said, wondering, though, how I was going to engineer you triggering a meeting with them.
"No – I don't want to do that – I'll be fine. And if I'm not, I can contact them then, can't I?" you announced.

After a short silence while we all considered how to react to this, Sarah responded "OK, my suggestion then, Alex, is that we prepare a 'Crisis Plan' – a written note of early warning signs that things are not right and what you know you can do to alleviate them. We can share this with the Aspire Team, to whom I will send your details, and if you find that you develop problems that you cannot manage again, you can contact them to seek help. I will give you their number. How does that sound?"

"That's fine" you replied – which I'm sure you felt it was, but I don't think I was the only one to doubt whether you would actually invoke their help if things deteriorated too much. I did manage to have a quiet word with Sarah afterwards, and she agreed with me an additional possible 'alert' trigger which was not strictly 'allowed' by the system, but could well be necessary: since my job enabled me to keep a watching brief on your progress in Leeds, we agreed that if I had any cause for concern, that I could contact her and she would ask the Aspire team to go round and check up on you. We were all concerned about how you would fare without the medication. She prepared the 'Crisis Plan' with you, and shared it with us at our last meeting with her before you would be returning to Leeds:

Early Warning Signs

- *Sleep disturbance – waking on numerous occasions through the night*

- *Losing the ability to focus on specific tasks*

- *Increased levels of irritability and anger*

- *Lots of thoughts going round in my head*

- *Increased feelings of anxiety*

- *Possible changes in facial expression*

- *Increased intensity to 'the voices'*

- *Less able to distract myself from the voices*

- *Feeling low in mood*

- *Altered ways of thinking that make me feel I am detached from reality*

- *Increased suspicion of others – people might be talking about me or might be watching/following me*

- *Feeling that I cannot trust other people*

- *Feeling that someone might harm me*

- *Guilt feelings concerning past events in my life that date back to my childhood*

- *Tendency to attach different meanings in comments made by others*

Crisis Plan

1. *Seek others out for company – this can be helpful as a reality check*

2. *Use of distraction techniques – listening to music, playing my guitar, reading*

3. *Access support networks if experiencing high levels of stress. This could be a range of people depending on the stressor – academic tutors at university, student*

counselling service, family members (brother, mother etc), friends, ASPIRE (Early Intervention Service in Leeds), or Sarah Scott (Sheffield Early Intervention Service)

4. Alex does not feel it would be helpful to have contact with ASPIRE, but does feel it would be useful to have a contact number if needed – 0113 200 9170

5. If Alex feels unable to access supportive contacts in Leeds he can contact Sarah Scott on 0114 271 6021 or 0787 068 0238

6. Alex has agreed that information can be sent to ASPIRE so that they are aware of his mental health difficulties and history

7. Visit the GP if Alex has any concerns about his mental health

8. Alex has previously found it difficult to ask for support at times when he is struggling with his mental health experiences. It is unlikely that he would ask for help if a crisis develops. Family, friends and mental health professionals may need to be proactive in helping Alex to seek and access support.

A Letter to My Son

And so, come September, and armed with your Crisis Plan, you gave notice at work and came in to Leeds with me to find a flat-share. I was pleased that you found one only a short walk from my office, and you had agreed to meet up regularly with Matthew and me after work for supper. However, two weeks into term, I met the two of you outside the Italian restaurant in Millennium Square, where we had enjoyed a couple of really good suppers last year. I'd reserved a table, but as we were sitting down, you looked really uncomfortable, and said "Mum, sorry, but this feels a bit crowded, can we go somewhere else?"

"OK, where would you like to go?" I replied.

"Actually, could we go somewhere out of town, where it will be quieter?" This was the first time, since that time outside my office where I finally identified paranoia as something of what you were suffering, that you articulated your preference for avoiding crowded places. I did not then realise that this would continue – and intensify – as a significant symptom of your condition.

Matthew and I exchanged a glance as I said "OK, let's find the car – do you have somewhere in mind?"

"Yes, we can go to this pub I used to go to on Sundays sometimes last year with the family who ran the pizza take-away in Adel. I know how to get there."

This was the first I'd heard of this. I knew you'd had a pizza delivery job last year, but as we drove out of the city, you explained that they were a really nice Persian family, who seemed to take a liking to you and invited you out on Sundays sometimes. How lovely, I thought, feeling a deep sense of gratitude to these people. Meanwhile, I found myself being directed off the main road to Otley, through Pool-in-Wharfedale, and across the moors.

"Alex, are we nearly there? I've got to get back to Sheffield after we've eaten."

"Yes, not far now Mum. Just turn left here."

So we joined the A59 heading towards Skipton, and shortly after you told me to pull up by a wayside pub just outside Blubberhouses – the Harper Lane Hotel.

At just after 6pm, the place was virtually deserted, so you had your wish for a quiet meal. Even here, though, you could not look the waiter directly in the eye, probably appearing to him decidedly shifty. On the way back to Leeds you asked me to stop by a reservoir so that you could have a cigarette, and Matthew joined you, while I sat in the car, worrying over how you might fare during this next year. Having dropped you both off in town, I did not get back home to Sheffield until nearly 9.30pm. Then fretted for an hour before going to bed and up again at 5.45am the next day for the drive to Leeds.

Dad had had an idea for how to minimise your reclusive tendencies so that they did not impinge too much on our Christmas celebrations that year. We would spend the holiday in our house in Grange-over-Sands, as we had done some years previously. There was a limited number of rooms for you to disappear into, and it would be warm and cosy. However, making this a reality was an anxious affair for me. I knew that, as always, you and Matthew would want to meet with your friends in Sheffield on Christmas Eve, so realistically, Dad would have to take you to Grange on Christmas morning, while I would travel up on Christmas Eve, taking the food and presents, and picking (auntie) Dot up from Bury en route.

You'll remember we had bought the house in Grange in 2000, as a base from which we could spend time with Gran, who still lived there on her own. We had all spent huge amounts of time there when you were younger, and Grandpa was still alive. But as she'd got older, we felt that it would be nicer for us to take the pressure off her 'hosting' our visits, and instead we could take her out for walks and meals without any hassle, and yet have a regular 'bolthole' for weekends away. 'Dormers' is a lovely cottagey house with sea-views from all windows on the south side of the house. Dad and I probably spent at least one weekend a month there, enjoying the proximity of the Lake District for hill-walks, a range of country restaurants for cosy Saturday night meals, and, for me, a mile-long promenade along which I would run from our house to pick up a Sunday paper. Remember that you, also, had enjoyed visiting the house on a couple of occasions for a weekend away with your friends from Sheffield. But you also probably did not remember the time that a stranger alerted me, on one bank holiday weekend staying with Gran and Grandpa when you were about eight, to the prospect of you and Matthew being engulfed by the treacherous quick-sands that were dotted around that part of Morecambe Bay. Unnoticed by me, reading, you had strayed further into the bay than was advisable, and I'd had to run down the beach to pull you both to safety. But we all remember, over the years, the convenient facility of the walk up to Hampsfell, which we could start straight from Dormers, and which – on the top – gave you a magnificent view of the Langdales, to the north, Ingleboro to the southeast, and the broad sweep of Morecambe Bay, across to Blackpool, to the south.

Dot and I arrived in Grange mid-afternoon, and Gran arrived to greet us shortly after. She and Dot helped me put up the decorations, before we had a light tea and then prepared the turkey and vegetables for the next day. I was already anxious because you had insisted you would get a late afternoon train to Sheffield on Christmas Eve – you might change your mind and not turn up? Dad had promised to ring when you arrived, and at eight o'clock I still had not heard. I could tell that Gran and Dot were starting to feel the tension even while we were all supposedly watching 'Scrooge' on the TV. At 9pm Dad called to say you'd arrived and we all breathed a sigh of relief. I asked that he try to get to Grange for one o'clock the next day.

In fact you all arrived at 2.15pm, but Dad had told me when you set off, so everything was planned properly. On arrival, you gave me a big hug, but then said you needed to have a quick walk to 'clear your head'. Five minutes later we all sat round with champagne and then had a lovely lunch, during which you seemed to relax a little. You even volunteered, afterwards, to hand round the presents from under the tree, but then, halfway through "Sorry – need to get some fresh air" you said, and out you went again. I felt the anxiety rise within me and also had to leave the room. I went upstairs to try to recover my composure, but couldn't stop the tears flowing. I kept hearing calls from downstairs, from Dad, Gran, Dot, "Come on, let's carry on…", and I wondered how they could just continue without missing a beat when you were so obviously troubled in our company. Only Matthew must have sensed the effect this was having on me. He came upstairs quietly and just sat next to me on the bed and put his arm round my shoulder. "Mum, I'm sure he'll be back soon."

You actually returned about an hour later, and we started the post-dinner Christmas games, and I thought that maybe, at last, you had settled into the occasion. But at ten o'clock, while we were watching television, you got up and announced you needed another walk. I followed you into the hall. "Alex, surely you can't need another walk. It's late, it's dark, why not wait till tomorrow morning – we've already arranged to walk round Tarn Howes tomorrow." This had to be another incidence of seriously impaired judgement – no-one in their right minds would take a 'long walk' at that time of night in Grange?
"No, Mum, I need a long walk now." And here it was again – that other recurring issue of limited parental influence over a 21-year-old – even where your judgement was clearly impaired – a long walk at 10pm in December? But how was I going to stop you?
"But where can you go at his time of night? There are no long walks with any light."
"Mum, I'll be fine – don't worry", as you turned and walked down the drive.
I stumbled back into the lounge "Andy – we can't let him go at this time of night – he doesn't know the area very well, and it's freezing!"
"He came back OK earlier, just let him be."

Gran took this opportunity to say she would go home, and so Dad disappeared to drive her, and Dot went up to bed. Matthew again tried to comfort me, and we settled down to watch a film. Two hours later there was no sign of you. Grange is a very small place. Where could you have walked to? There are many fell walks, but impossible to negotiate in the dark. Or were they? Could you be sitting somewhere high on a dark fell, in the freezing cold, perhaps with a razor in your pocket? Once I started articulating my fears, it did not take long to instil the same sense of dread in Dad. We agreed to go and look for you. Dad would drive systematically along all the roads in and out of town, while I would take a torch and walk the length of the promenade. It was very eerie, edging along the promenade at one o'clock on Boxing Day morning. Holding the torch in front of me while calling your name, I kept thinking I could see something move, but in reality there were just shadows. Dad arrived back a little after me, and had similarly had no joy. So, where could you be at nearly two o'clock?

Matthew had fallen asleep on the couch, and we joined him to watch yet another film, just to keep us occupied. But neither of us could really concentrate. I told Dad I was going to find the emergency number for local social services, and he said he was going to drive a long way along each of the four main roads out of town, in turn, to see if he could find you. I eventually got through to Cumbria County Council's emergency number, and, having explained your recent mental health history and the current circumstances, they suggested that I should ring the police, alerting them to a missing person. This seemed incredibly serious, and I didn't want to bring you to their attention, but what else could I do? And I didn't know then, that this was an action I would need to repeat over the years. They took the details, asked a few questions and informed me that someone would be with us in the next hour or so.

Dad arrived back, empty-handed, just before the police arrived. There was a man and a woman, and they asked me to escort them around the property, as standard practice was to make sure that the person was not hidden somewhere. So, rather surreally, I took them upstairs, explaining that Dot was asleep in one of the bedrooms, and then outside to open the garage and the workshop. Then we all sat down, while they took formal statements from Dad and me.
"Mrs Holt, is there nowhere you can think of where Alex might have gone?" the senior officer asked.
"No – he hasn't been up here that often recently, and really doesn't know his way around that well. The only person he knows here is his Gran, and she was with us all evening."
"We've put out a call to all the stations within thirty miles, together with Alex's description, and our colleagues are

currently checking out the hospitals, and there is no information as yet."

There followed routine conversations about Alex's recent troubled history, interspersed with occasional messages through on the intercom from police colleagues. Then "We think we've had a sighting" the officer said while covering the intercom with his hand.

"Whereabouts? OK."

A smile, then "Well, it seems a colleague who was on his way to his early shift has just seen someone like Alex walking down Windermere Road. He's going to pick him up and will be here in a few minutes." It was by then 6.30am. Sure enough, five minutes later, you emerged from a police car and we both rushed out to meet you. Hugs. Then much commotion as everyone wanted to know where you'd been the last eight or nine hours in the freezing cold.

"Just walking along roads. It helps", you said, simply. For over eight hours in the dark?

After the police had gone, things deteriorated.

"What the hell do you think you've been doing, Alex?" shouted Dad, "We've been worried sick. Mum's been walking along the promenade in the dark, and I've been driving half the night looking for you."

"I just needed some space, some air…"

"Oh, well that's all right then."

You were close up, shouting at each other and I couldn't bear it. I came between you to push you apart, wondering what Dot would be making of all this upstairs in her room. The shouting continued until Dad stormed off outside with the parting comment "If this carries on I'm going to outlive you."

You asked me if we could go for a drive, to calm down. Why not? So we set off back up Windermere Road towards Bowness. We didn't talk that much.

"I don't have much conversation, Mum, but I enjoy your company."

"And I yours, Alex, but you really need to be more communicative, and more responsible about your actions. We want to help, but can't do anything if you just disappear without explanation."

"I'm sorry, Mum. I'll make it up to you. I love you."

I suppressed the tears and gave him a weak smile. We were on our way back to Grange as you had decided you'd like a walk along the promenade. By this time you were hungry, and we had a full English at the promenade café.

"Can you drive me back to Sheffield – I don't want to stay here any longer?"

"Yes, of course, but we'll need to pack up our things and I'll need to take Dot home en route."

"OK, well can I get the train to Leeds then instead?

"I don't know whether they'll be running from here on Boxing Day, let's check."A quick look on my phone suggested that on a normal day there was a train to Leeds from Kendal at 11.30am, so we set off. However, the station was shut for Boxing Day, so we drove round the corner to the bus station to find there was a bus leaving at midday.

By this time, thinking of you deserting us again back to Leeds on your own, I couldn't prevent revealing my thoughts.

"Alex, I don't want you to be on your own again in that flat in Leeds. Why can't you come back with us to Sheffield for the rest of the holiday?"

"I will come back in a day or two. I just need to pick up some books for studying. Just relax, you've got nothing to lose."

"I don't want to lose you", I say, shakily.

"You're not going to – I'm going to be around always. I'll ring you tomorrow morning", and with that, a kiss and you were gone.

It was a difficult drive back to Grange. I had to keep my feelings in check and try to be as calm and composed as possible to deal with the situation. Dad had rung Gran to explain that we would not, after all, be going up to Tarn Howes for a walk, so she had come round to help with whatever was going to happen, and Dot was sitting reading in the lounge, looking uneasy. Matthew had just woken up. I announced that we would go back to Sheffield early, and it was all hands on deck to pack up everything. Matthew and I set off first with Dot, whom we deposited back in Bury, with Dad following on in the other car, tasked with the final clearing up.

The next morning, a Wednesday, there was no phone call. At midday I rang you but your phone went straight to voicemail. How were you? I went to play racket-ball at 6.45pm, and you rang from Sheffield station. I told you to ring Dad for a lift home, feeling incredibly relieved that you would be back home for a while. Those next few days, you spent much of the time in bed, interspersed with visits to your friend Richard G.

Dad and I agreed that you should not go back to Leeds – not much studying was happening, you probably weren't going to many lectures, and generally could not relate to people outside the family. So one morning we both went up to your room together to have a talk about this.
"Alex, why don't you stay at home for a while? We can contact the university and ask for however much sick leave you need to get back on your feet." I suggested.
"Why are you bothered about me?" you replied after a while. "What have I ever done for you? I've never given you anything but disrespect." Neither of us knew what you meant by this, beyond a few angry words recently. And then you cried – and we tried not to cry with you, while giving you reassuring hugs.

But we were unable to persuade you to stay. So here we were again, recognising your impaired judgement, yet having limited influence over you now, as a 21-year-old, to reconsider. And though you kept deferring your return to Leeds, I dropped you off on the campus on the second day of the new term, with you promising to present yourself to a doctor about keeping well, and also talk to your tutor about your predicament. I rang the Business School myself, asking if I could meet with your tutor to discuss your progress and explain what was going on, to be told – yet again – that they could not discuss your work without your consent.

And so continued the rest of your year. I tried to keep an eye on you in your flat, and twice had to ask the Aspire team to go and check on you when I could get no answer. You insisted with them that you did not need their help, so what could they do? I kept in touch with Sarah from the Sheffield Early Intervention Team to ask her advice on occasions, and she was always very responsive and helpful, but could not, obviously, actually do anything either. At one stage I noticed your car had disappeared from the road and I found out that you'd had to sell it for scrap as it had finally packed up. We had several more trips out to Blubberhouses for tea, and each time you would ask me to drop you off around the corner from your flat, not wanting me to be seen outside. I would glance back at the way you would walk off shiftily, with your collar up, and then I would try to stifle the tears driving back to Sheffield.

You spent the Easter holiday at home, accompanied by your books, and assured us you were up to speed with your studies. You seemed less troubled than at Christmas, and saw a little of your friends. However, of course, the inevitable happened. It was late May and I'd checked the date when your final results would be published, and went to the university notice-board where they would be displayed, not far from my office. Your name did not feature. I found out later that the reason you were not mentioned as a 'fail' was because you had not actually presented yourself for the exams. It occurred to me, ruefully, that we had funded two degree courses at Leeds University, and that neither of them was going to yield a result – Matthew had decided after Christmas not to complete his music degree there, as it was not to his liking, but had not told us of this decision until a few weeks ago when he had been offered a place at Westminster University for a Commercial Music degree course the following autumn, and had got himself a job at the Norwich Union in Leeds until then.

6. "I Just Need a Job" – June 2007 to March 2009

So that was that. We collected you and your things and settled you back at home. You insisted that you'd be fine once you got a job – that was all you needed to get back into the swing of things. On the face of it you were well placed for this, with your good A levels and extensive and varied work experience, and with positive references available from John Lewis and two different hospitals. A morning spent online and you had a long list of applications to make. You looked motivated, and Dad moved into gear, taking you off to the shops to get a suit and some smart clothes and accessories. Invitations to interview came thick and fast. Yet three weeks – and about six or seven interviews – later, it was clear that something was not working.

"It's not going to happen, is it?" I said to Dad one morning before you were up. "If I were on the interview panel, I would be wary about Alex – there is just something about the way he presents which does not seem quite normal. Is he over-anxious? Too intense? I can't put my finger on it but when you have an extended conversation with him you can tell he is not at all comfortable."

"Yes, you're right. There's not much we can do about that though."

"No, maybe Sarah could offer some advice – I'll give her a ring and see." All Sarah could say was that, in time, you may be able to control your anxieties enough to be able to present more normally.

Were you – how were you – going to resume a normal life? We had no answers, and our worries were growing. We had an uncertain prognosis on your mental condition – psychosis, or maybe something even worse – but had been told that there was no 'quick fix'. You were absolutely convinced that if you got a job you would be able to cope again – and you might have – but your condition militated against this possibility. And you and we both recognised the need for your independence from us and the family home, but how was that to be achieved?

You continued with your job-seeking efforts while we went on a touring holiday across Europe, and in frequent calls home, you seemed to be able to maintain reasonably high spirits. But on our return, you announced your plan to go down to London to seek work.

"There are lots more jobs going down there, Mum, and my friend Paul has offered to let me sleep on his couch for a few weeks."

"Who is Paul? I don't remember hearing about him" I replied.

"He was on my course and we stayed in touch. He's working at Price Waterhouse in London now."

"OK – if you think you can manage all right on your own?"

"Yes, I'll be fine – if you can lend me some money to get there and pay for my keep?" After the first rash of unsuccessful interviews, you had signed on for benefit, but nothing had come through yet.

You went, but six weeks later you were back with another plan.

"I'm going to Edinburgh to try up there. Richard G's working there at the moment, so I can keep him company while trying for jobs."

"Alex, it's not working. Why do you think Edinburgh will be any better than Sheffield or London?" Dad inquired.

"I don't know, but I have to try. I NEED to try, Dad. I will get a job." Dad couldn't offer you any alternative, and neither could I. So off to Edinburgh you went. Again, numerous telephone conversations, while confirming no work had transpired, suggested that you were reasonably happy, and meeting people. You were renting a little bedsit in Leith, from a landlady who just seemed to have taken you under her wing, and you described how Leith was a bit like a holiday resort, with its own promenade, apparently. But the plan ended in the same way – you were back in Sheffield by September, and we all had to think again. You were downhearted by this time, and not looking forward to being once again dependent on living with us.

Your other friend Richard J had been a postman in Sheffield since leaving university. He had just bought his own house on the Manor, and had suggested that you could move in with him, contributing rent towards his mortgage. This seemed a good idea all around, and you moved in with him in October. By this time, however, you had given up on job applications, and the benefits office was not coming up with any suggestions for you. At least you had some independence from us, though, and I remember that we all managed to have a really good Christmas that year, as you fully engaged in all the usual activities. You already found it difficult to smile, however, and Dad had to try really hard to produce one from you when taking the required family photos.

But again, it did not last. One evening in February, I took a call from Richard J.

"I'm really sorry, Gill, but I've had to ask Alex to leave – I can't take it any more."

"Oh dear, what's happened?" I responded, heart sinking.

"I got home from work tonight, and the lounge carpet is an absolute disaster. He'd spilled some stuff all over it and tried to clean it up but made it much worse. He's just left."

"Sorry, Richard. You go and get a new carpet, and send me the bill. Has Alex taken his things?"

"No – he left in a huff."

"OK, I'll come and pick them up. I'll be there in a half an hour or so."

I rang your number, but it went straight to voicemail, so left a message saying I was going to pick up your belongings. When I returned from Richard's you were still not back, so I rang again – voicemail again. With no sign of you by 11.30pm, I was worried.

"Where can he be till this time? He'll be upset – I hope he doesn't do anything stupid"

Dad replied reassuringly "I'm sure he'll be home soon." I went to bed with a heavy heart.

I woke up to find out you had not come home. I rang Richard J to see if you had returned there, but no. I rang Richard G to see if you had turned up there – no again. Neither Dad nor I could think of anywhere else you might be so there was no choice but to report you missing. The officer arrived mid-morning and took further details of your recent movements. He asked where you might go if you'd strayed beyond Sheffield. We explained that you were familiar with Leeds as you had been to university there, and that there was a connection with Grange-over-Sands, through your Gran, but she would have rung had you gone up there. He said he'd keep us apprised of any developments. But where were you Alex? The weather was still wintry, and you had little money, so where had you slept last night? We rang Sarah to see if she or any colleagues had heard from you, but they hadn't. The day dragged by and all the police could tell us was that they had distributed your description with an alert to all staff in Sheffield and Leeds. Again I imagined you sitting somewhere alone with a razor in your hand, wondering if you could try again.

We spent the next morning in tense silence, listening out for any call that might be the police with news of you. The only call was from Sarah asking if we had heard yet. Then, around lunchtime, Dad looked out of the conservatory window and said "Of course", before dashing out of the back door and round the corner of the garden. Five minutes later he re-emerged, pushing you through the door before him. "I thought I could smell cigarette smoke, and couldn't work out where it was coming from, but it was Alex – in the garden cellar!" he announced. (There is an underground store beneath the corner of our garden). You were half asleep and wet through and your big parka was virtually dripping (as water seeps down to the cellar from our patio). "Alex, how long have you been down there, we've been worried sick about you?" I asked, trying to sound a bit cross above the intense relief I was actually feeling.
"Only since last night" you said, wearily.
"So where were you the night before, after you left Richard J's?"
"I went up to Leeds. "
"Why?"
"Because I needed to get away. I'd messed up my relationship with my best friend."
"So where did you sleep?
"On a park bench."
"Oh Alex, you'll make yourself ill. You look dreadful. Why don't you take those clothes off, have a warm bath and go to bed for a while."
We rang the police to report your return and they came to check up on your story before you went for a lie down. Dad

and I took stock of the situation. You were now nearly twenty-five years old, with no degree, no job; you had upset your best friend, and most of your other friends had lost touch with you; and you had now been reported twice to the police as a missing person. Where to from here?

That Spring was a particularly difficult time for all of us. My Auntie Dot in Bury had become ill, and I had been going over there at weekends, helping her to settle into supported housing. One night I arrived home from work to find you saying you felt very anxious, and thought you may need to check yourself into Chester Ward for some support. While I was talking to the staff there on the phone, Dad took a call from Dot's supported housing, saying that she had fallen, for the second time, in her new flat, and had been taken to Bury General hospital. So we agreed that Dad would go over to Bury and see Dot, and I would sort out your situation. It turned out that the team could not find any beds available in Sheffield, but told us there was one in Worksop, if we could get you there.

So here was another issue – a rare occasion when you had the self-awareness and sound judgement to seek support from 'the system', and it could not deliver. Worksop is nearly thirty miles from Sheffield. I could get you there, but would you be prepared to go that far? If you had been on your own without our support it would have been impossible to get there realistically on public transport. If that had been the case, would they have offered to transport you there?

However, you agreed to go, so we set off at around 7.30pm for Worksop. We chatted all the way, me asking what it was that was troubling you, and you finding it difficult to explain. I could tell that you were not completely convinced that this was the right move, so was not surprised when you asked if we could stop for you to have a cigarette at some stage. We arrived at the hospital at about 9pm and sat down in reception while the charge nurse asked endless questions about your history. You were getting agitated at this apparent bureaucracy, and so it was no surprise when you announced, after about twenty minutes, that you did not want to stay at the hospital after all. So we drove home, and found Dad had just arrived back from Bury, having seen Dot.

I went to work the next day, leaving him to sort out how you were feeling and what to do about Dot, who would be undergoing a series of tests to see what was wrong.

It turned out Dot had cancer, which was quite well developed, and so would need nursing home care, once she was stable enough to be discharged. So after a full week's work, driving to Leeds and back each day, I was then driving over the Snake Pass to Bury Royal Infirmary to see Dot. Dad was very helpful, in appreciating that the last thing I needed was that drive, so for a few Sundays he would drive me over and read the paper in the car while I sat with Dot. A few weeks later, we arranged for Dot to be ambulanced over to Sheffield to the nursing home next door to us.

Meanwhile, you were at home with us again and very restless, wondering how you could set your life back on some kind of positive track. You were back into a routine, on medication under the supervision of the Early Intervention Team via Sarah, whom you were seeing once a week, usually choosing to go for a drive out to a coffee shop in Hope. You were now regularly on anti-psychotic medication, at her suggestion, but not at all happy about it. And it didn't seem to us that there was anything in train to move you forward, support your 'recovery' – a term that was regularly used as the intended destination, but for which there seemed to be no obvious reliable pathway.
"Where's this all leading?" Dad asked me one day, after Sarah had picked you up for your weekly appointment. "How is going for a chat and a coffee every week going to help Alex get better?"
"Well, it gives him a chance to talk to someone who can relate to how he's feeling, and who knows what kind of help he needs."
"Well that's not quite true is it? Sarah has just about admitted in our previous discussions that she – they – can't give us a prognosis on how, when, if he's going to get better at any stage. She's more or less told us that we should be pleased that they've managed to keep him alive so far."
In fact, Sarah had told us that she should really have passed you over to the Community Health Team, as support from her Early Intervention Team was supposed to be limited to

the first two years of 'intensive' support, before settling into a more routine support system, but that she was staying with you longer, on the pretext to the authorities of the unhelpful break in Leeds, and thinking that you trusted her and she could help you more. At this stage we had not heard of a 'Community Care Plan', but if we had, it would have been clear that they did not have one for you at that time.

However, your state of anxiety, which had prompted the visit to Worksop, continued, and developed such that Sarah organised for you to have a spell in Chester Ward at the end of April. At that stage we received the news that they had decided a worse diagnosis for you – they thought you had paranoid schizophrenia – even worse than psychosis! We never quite worked out the difference between these two, other than schizophrenia was like a whole bundle of psychotic symptoms rather than just the one of having delusions. We had a case meeting with Sarah and the staff while you were there, at which it was agreed to adjust your medication. They agreed we could take you out for a meal into Derbyshire on your birthday, but neither Dad nor I felt any real cause for celebration...

The rest of 2008 drifted by with no significant developments in relation to your condition. Dad and I had a touring holiday in Canada in July. Dot died and we had her funeral in August. Matthew worked in London through the summer holiday, but came back for a couple of weekends and you enjoyed having his company. Your weekly sessions with Sarah continued and I maintained communication with her by phone. She agreed with me that it would help for you to have your own place, and so she had submitted an application on your behalf for supported housing from an organisation called Halfway Housing. It took till January, however, before they came up with a potential tenancy, available for occupation from March.

You were looking forward to having your own place, and it was a nice enough studio flat in City Road across town. But you obviously felt slightly anxious about living independently again, after all that time at home, and twice, when Dad took you over there, and installed your household goods, you asked to defer staying over for a few days. So, by the time we were due to fly to Morocco for a week's holiday in mid-March, you were still at home with us. You had agreed to stay much of the time in our house, anyway, for the week we were away to look after Squeak the cat – this had been a regular job for you while we had been away on holiday in recent years. However, I arrived home from work on the Thursday evening to find you feeling decidedly edgy, and we were concerned about leaving you in that state. It was too late to speak with Sarah by this time, to ask that she keep an eye on you, so asked our friend John to come over and have a word. His daughter had had mental health problems for some years longer than you, so he understood the situation and was used to supporting her through fragile periods. We explained that we would ring Sarah from Marrakesh airport the next morning, so that she could check up on you, and that John would also check on how things were going later in the day. You said that was OK but we could tell you were very anxious, as you went back upstairs.

"I don't think we ought to go", Dad said. Before I could reflect on this, my immediate – selfish – reaction to this announcement was disappointment. Work had been very challenging in the previous weeks, and I had been really looking forward to a relaxing break. But as I was thinking about it John interjected.

"But you can't stop all your plans every time Alex feels unwell. If we'd done that with Rosa, we wouldn't have been doing much these last few years. I'll make sure he's all right, so don't worry."

We took his advice, but it didn't stop us worrying. We had a really early start to the airport the next morning, and so did not get much feel for how you were when we said goodbye to you, still in bed.

In retrospect, however, this was probably the biggest turning point of your – and our – journey since your first attempt at taking your life. We were about to find out how the mental health support system could not be relied upon to support you in all crisis situations when we were absent – you were always going to have problems relying on staff who were only available 9-5; that we could not expect a seamless service between the mental health and A and E wings of the

NHS; that the police were the last port of call for those who fell between the numerous 'stools'; and that the rigidity of the legal aspects of the system would not accede readily to the insight and support offered by family and caring friends. But, most significantly, that it was important that one of us was on call 24-7 if we were to have any chance of keeping you safe. This we managed to do over the coming difficult years, but wondered what happened to the dozens of similar sufferers whom we met on Chester Ward and elsewhere who had no relatives or 'significant others' to support them through such frightening experiences.

While Dad was taking care of the admin for the hire car at Marrakesh airport, I got through to Sarah's office, only to be told that she was on annual leave that day. So I explained the situation, and asked that one of the team could go round to see how you were and, if necessary, give support over the weekend. The guy who answered was unsure about the wisdom of this as he thought that someone unknown to you turning up at the door might cause you more distress than comfort. But he said he'd see what he could do. Concerned that this sounded unhelpful, I rang John, who agreed to go round and check up on you. He rang an hour or so later to say that you had seemed OK and had agreed to have tea with them that evening – John would pick you up at about seven o'clock.

"That's not going to happen," said Dad when I relayed this information to him, sitting at a café having some lunch. "There's no way he's going to agree to eat with them, when he's hardly seen them since he's been ill."

"Well, at least John will be back later and have a conversation with him" I replied, thinking that if anything seemed wrong, John would know what to do – we had left him all the relevant numbers.

We set off in our car towards Essaouira on the coast, a three-hour road trip, during which I realised I had lost the phone signal. When we arrived at our Riad, at about seven o'clock, I found that I had two missed calls and two voicemail messages on my phone. I was frustrated to find that I could not pick up the voicemails as I did not know the code for foreign pick-up. But I recognised the numbers – one was the Early Intervention Service and the other John. Oh dear!

I rang The Early Intervention Team first, but of course there was no response as the office would by then be closed. Next John informed me that he had just been round to collect you, but that there was no answer. So I rang you and, unusually, you picked up the call instantly.

"Hi Alex. We're in Morocco now – how are you?"

""Not good, I'm in an ambulance on the way to hospital."

"Oh no, what's the matter?"

"I've got chest pains, so the Team thought I should go to A and E."

"Is there someone with you whom I could speak with?" I needed to have a clearer idea of what was happening here. A bit of a shuffling noise and then:

"Hello, Mrs Holt? This is Jean, and I'm accompanying Alex to A and E. The mental health team had visited Alex earlier and called for an ambulance when he was complaining about pains in his chest. He says he still has them, but seems OK to us at present."

"Oh. Hasn't one of them come with him to see what happens?"

"No, there was no suggestion that they would come with him."

"Right, we've just arrived in Morocco, but how can I check on what happens?"

"We're nearly there now, so I suggest you ring them up to check on the outcome in about forty-five minutes time", and she gave me the number.

"Right, thank you. Please tell Alex I'll also ring him again to see how he is."

"Of course. Goodbye now."

She sounded a very caring person, and I felt reassured that she was with you. But at the same time I was becoming exasperated by the telephone technology – the signal had been fading in and out through these exchanges, even though I was hanging over the edge of the hotel balcony to try to improve it. I was annoyed that the Team had been unable to get through to me earlier, and I had not managed to talk with them, but felt incensed that a Team member could not have accompanied you to hospital. However, I took the opportunity to convey this information to John, who told me he and Diana would set off for the hospital to check what was happening, and they would ring once they had news. By this stage Dad, who had taken charge of the driving from Marrakesh, and after a very early start and flight, was fast asleep in bed, and there was no point in waking him just to worry alongside me.

So, another phone call.
"Hello, I'm ringing to check on Alex Holt, who came in by ambulance a while ago. He was complaining of chest pains."
"Who am I speaking to?"
"I'm his mother."
OK, I'll get the charge nurse."
"Hello Mrs Holt. We discharged Alex a while ago as there was no problem with his chest."
"But what was he like? He has mental health issues and I think it might be that that is troubling him rather than his chest."
"Yes, I did notice he seemed troubled, but we had to discharge him as he was physically fit. I was worried about how he would be so I rang the police to look out for him."
Did she really say that?! No point in continuing this conversation, I needed to find out where – and how – you were.
Again you answered your phone immediately.
"Where are you Alex?"
"I'm just walking down the main road from the hospital, but I'm cold as I have no coat and it's raining. Also, I've got no money on me for the bus."
How could they let you leave the hospital like that? How could the Team have sent you to hospital so ill-prepared? I was becoming quite incensed by now, at least as angry as I was worried.
"OK. John and Diana are on their way, so tell me where you are and they can pick you up."
"I'll just find a sign ... here we are – I'm on Barnsley Road."
"That's very long, you need to find a side road and stay on the corner so that John will know where you are."
"Right, I'm on the corner of Norwood Road now."

"OK, Alex, I'm going to ring John now and tell him. Don't move, will you, till he gets there? I'll ring you back anyway after I've spoken with him."
"Hi John."
"It's Diana, Gill, John's driving. We're nearly at the Northern General now. Have you heard how Alex is."
She couldn't believe what I told her, of course, but told me not to worry as they would be with you quite quickly now.
"Hi Alex. John will be there in a few minutes."
"Too late, Mum, the police are taking me back to the hospital. We're just going into the car park now."
"What?! OK, I'll have to ring John again, and he'll come in and sort things out – don't worry."
"OK."

By this time I was completely stressed out and on the verge of tears. The whole situation seemed surreal. Yes, Dad and I didn't understand how to deal with your troubled mind, but surely hospital staff should be able to ensure you were looked after properly? Why should the police have to be involved – you hadn't done anything wrong? Anyone would think you were a criminal.

When I rang him yet again, John agreed how preposterous it was, and headed off for the hospital, promising to ring once he knew what was happening. But when he rang back, about an hour and a half later, the situation had deteriorated further. The police had taken you to the mental health wing of the hospital, where staff had assessed you and deemed you too unwell to go home. When John arrived and heard all this he said that he could take you home with them, as I had asked him to look out for you while I was away. But they said that he had no status in relation to your welfare and that you would have to stay in one of the wards there. They did agree, however, to see if they could find a bed in Chester or one of the other wards at the local Michael Carlisle Centre to transfer you to. John and I could not conceive of why the A and E staff would not liaise with them. However, he said that he and Diana would go back to the hospital the next day to see what would happen. I thanked him and said we would be back as soon as we could get a flight and would let them know.

By this time it was nearly one in the morning and I was exhausted from my 5am start from Sheffield to Manchester airport, and three hours of stressful phone discussions, continuously interrupted by signal loss. I woke Dad to explain the sorry saga, and suggested he take over the reins to find a flight home, and contact the travel company to cancel the rest of our itinerary for the week.

When I awoke at around 7.30am, he had booked a flight back on the Sunday morning, but we had to wait till the travel company opened for business to sort out the rest. We had a word with the owner/manager of the Riad to explain our situation and he was very helpful. The travel company also, were incredibly efficient. By 9.30am they had cancelled everything and booked alternative accommodation in Marrakesh for overnight Saturday/Sunday prior to our morning flight.

We then had the surreal experience of trying to enjoy some relaxation ahead of our three-hour road trip back to Marrakesh that afternoon. I can see it now, Alex – sitting on the rooftop of the riad, sipping mint tea in the warm sunshine, looking out to sea and listening to the eerie sound of the call to prayers from several mosques – both of us wishing we hadn't continued with our holiday plans in the face of your anxiety.
"That's it" Dad announced "We're never going to both be away together until we know Alex is better." I nodded in silent agreement, and indeed, for the next five years, the longest the two of us were away together was for a four-day weekend in Paris and a five-day trip to Tenby to celebrate my sixtieth birthday with friends. Those two days in Morocco signalled a significant shift in the way we would organise our life – whatever happened, one of us would always be there for you.

We were so grateful to John and Diana. We had been in phone contact and they had been to see you at the Northern General on Saturday and told us that the Team had found you a bed back at the Michael Carlisle Centre from Sunday. We went straight there from Manchester Airport on Sunday afternoon and found you, remarkably, dismayed and bewildered about your experience, rather than anxious or angry. A meeting had been organised with Sarah for the following morning to decide what happened next. I rang John to thank him and invite them out for a meal to show our appreciation. Even you, Alex, in your vulnerable state, vocalised how kind they had been in supporting you in our absence. We were so lucky to have friends involved who had experience of this hitherto unknown world of mental illness.

And it was a new world we were entering, Alex, all of us. You, of course, primarily, but with Dad and I fussing round the edges of your experience, looking on with horror, not knowing what to do, and getting things wrong sometimes. And Matthew coming home from London on occasions, never knowing how you would be: would you be in a settled period, able to spend brotherly time with him at home, going to the pub, listening to music together?; or would you have been neglecting your medication, and he might visit you in hospital – an experience which none of us could have imagined how distressing it would be to begin with but which we would become increasingly blasé about over the next few years.

Yes, looking back, Alex, that was the occasion when we realised just what a fight you – and we in your support – had on our hands. Our family was at war with an invisible but present and terrifying force which none of us understood or had any knowledge of how to deal with. I wonder whether you felt that was a key milestone, or perhaps you had long since felt the overwhelming powerlessness that was now overtaking us?

7. Home and Away, a Revolving Door – March

2009 to August 2011

Everyone – including you – agreed that getting you settled into your own flat was important. With the support of a 'key worker', you would be able to be independent again, and start to build back your confidence and 'do things'. So, how to bring that about? The case conference! Three days after our return from Morocco there were nine of us in a room at the Michael Carlisle Centre's Chester Ward – that is you, Dad and I with six professionals – psychiatrist, psychologist, senior ward nurse, your allocated nurse, a student nurse, and Sarah, your social worker from the Team. Bearing in mind one of your serious anxieties was being in the company of too many people, I always wondered why it was necessary to keep putting you through this process over the years. You never looked comfortable – why would you? As usual, the outcome included agreement on refinements to your medication and on the timescale for keeping you on the ward and then gradually allowing extended periods away to ultimately full discharge. Given your earlier anxiety about moving to the flat, we all agreed that you should spend a week or so with us before moving in there.

Years ago in my first job as a town planner I had known of, and dealt with, issues around the 'Community Care' notion. This was introduced in the 1970s and 80s as a more effective means of supporting vulnerable people – the elderly, disabled and mentally ill – in supportive home-based environments, rather than hospitalising them for extensive periods. I had been involved in planning the provision of such supportive housing. I was now about to find out what this could be like in practice, in the twenty-first century.

As originally planned several weeks earlier, Dad helped you move into your new flat while I was at work. We both visited you the following Saturday and were impressed with what we saw – it seemed the kind of place where you could re-find your independence in a pleasant and potentially supportive environment. It was one of a block of eight purpose-built flats in a relatively new development squeezed into a long run of old terraced houses on City Road, just a short walk from the city centre, and an even shorter one to Norfolk Park. That first Saturday we all went for a walk through the park and had a coffee, looking down at the view over the city made famous in 'The Full Monty'. This set the scene for I can't remember how many Saturday mornings when I would drive over and either we would go for a walk and a coffee, or I would bring you back to ours for the weekend, often involving watching a Liverpool match on Sky Sports.

You seemed quite settled in City Road. The flat was small but cosy, and we could tell you felt pleased to have your own place. Your assigned key worker would visit you twice a week to check on how you were and soon you were involved, with him, in a walking group, and on occasional visits to the cinema. You also sometimes went for a pint to the 'local' with one of the fellow tenants. This had to be good for redeveloping your social skills and also keeping you more active? We discussed getting you a bike for Christmas to give you more flexibility for getting out and about. But this settled period came to an end after about six months.

We had been pleased that you seemed to have developed a friendship with one of your fellow tenants. However, this apparently positive development started to be the source of concern. One Saturday morning you let slip that you had lent him quite a large sum of money which had yet to be repaid. "Alex, that is not a good idea. You don't have much yourself, and you can't afford to help him out" At this stage you were on Income Support, and it seemed likely so was he.
"Well, I always give something to the 'Big Issue' guys, so it's just the same, helping someone out."
"But has he said when he'll pay you back?"
"Yes, when his benefit cheque comes in."
"Well, make sure he does, and don't do it again, Alex, it's really not a good idea."

Dad and I felt very unsettled by this revelation and, so it proved, justifiably. About ten days later our phone rang, early in the morning while we were still in bed.

"Hello" said Dad, very groggily, and then "WHAT?!" he shouted.

It seemed your 'friend' had entered your room at night and stolen your computer – or so you thought. This situation would be distressing for anyone, but it really ratcheted up your paranoia. Dad agreed to go over and sort it out as I had to leave for work shortly. In tandem with the housing association landlord, Dad reported the incident to the police who came to investigate. They found no proof of your assertion but did uncover some surprising information – your fellow tenant had had a history of petty theft, which the housing association had failed to discover when checking him out prior to granting the tenancy. But with no proof they had no grounds to evict him so everyone agreed that you needed to move elsewhere to feel more secure. Dad bought you a new computer.

"But why do I have to move? I like it here, and it's him that's caused the problem?" you cried. A good question, but unfortunately there was no alternative, and also nowhere for you to move to immediately, so you came back home with us until the housing association could find you a new tenancy.

A few weeks later you moved into a new flat, closer to the family home. It was a large bedsit on the second floor of a large old terraced house, and you had more room than before. However, there was no common room for socialising, and we became concerned that you were turning in on yourself, becoming more reclusive again as you had in Leeds. We also had a shock one Sunday morning when we went to visit you to be told you had received a letter from your bank, threatening legal action if you did not sort out the unplanned overdraft – of around £600 – immediately.

"How on earth have you managed to get into so much debt?", said Dad when you showed him the letter.

"I've been gambling online. I was doing well to begin with then everything went pear-shaped."

"Alex, that really is pathetic – you know that's a mug's game, you're not that gullible."

"Yes, I know Dad. I'm sorry, and I won't do it again, I promise."

You didn't, but we became increasingly worried about how reclusive you were becoming once again. You rarely contacted us and often did not respond to calls or texts, and twice one of us had called round on spec to receive no response, but thought we could see lights in your flat. So Dad went round one Sunday night having sent a message that he was coming to visit and would not leave your flat until he had spoken with you. He ended up having to get the police round to help him check on your welfare.

We informed Sarah of this incident, and she was concerned on her visit to you shortly after that you were harbouring thoughts of throwing yourself from the window. Apparently you admitted to having stopped taking the medication, having suicidal thoughts, and agreed with her suggestion for another spell in hospital to settle you back into routine. By now it was leading up to Christmas, and so after ten days or so, Chester Ward gave you home leave for a few days, during which we managed to have a reasonably normal and enjoyable time with Matthew and Gran.

At your discharge this time, it was agreed that you would benefit from fully supported housing (that is, 24-hour staffing), but that there were no vacancies in the city at that time. Sarah advised that the Beaufort Road site in Broomhill, only a couple of miles from our house, would be ideal and so you joined its waiting list. We did not know then that this fact alone was to be the most critical factor in denying you the possibility of settling into an appropriate and supported setting in 'the community' for the next three years. The shortage of suitable accommodation for such a large city was evident, but also you never seemed to rise to the top of the waiting list for what was available. Later we would wonder if, perhaps, you attracted less priority than others in your situation because the authorities knew that if all else failed, you could always be cared for under our roof.

Sarah thought that you would benefit from moving to a shared house tenancy – in which you would share both kitchen and living room with four other tenants, and so there would be plenty of scope for socialising, and you would continue to have key worker support. There was a space in one coming up in the next few weeks, and while you waited for it to become available, we settled once again into family living at home.

Dad worked from home so saw more of you than did I, who was still working full-time in Leeds, so during the week, you remained mostly reliant on Dad for company, regularly going out for coffees and having walks occasionally, although he did sometimes take you to your friend, Richard G's in Dore. As I would continue to do for the next few years, I was determined to have holiday breaks, and in February 2010 I went with my friend Hilary for a week to Barbados, a welcome break from my challenging job in Leeds. It was also a break, of course, from caring responsibilities for you, Alex, and I was acutely aware that this left Dad alone in this. Every evening I texted you (with limited response as usual) and e-mailed Dad, who told me everything was fine and to stop contacting him as there was no point in going away for a break if I was asking after you every day. However, on my return home I discovered that, in fact, your condition had deteriorated, since you had stopped the medication once more, and Dad had found you in the cellar trying to cut yourself with a kitchen knife. This prompted another spell in hospital to stabilise your medication once more, and by this time you were able to be discharged into your new shared house.

The house in Carterknowle Road suited you and seemed to work for a while. You related well to the other tenants, and re-engaged with walking and cinema visits with your key worker, who visited twice a week. The location was well placed for visits with both us and your friend Richard G, and you had found another fellow tenant with whom to have an occasional beer. You were still having fortnightly trips into Derbyshire with Sarah, and by the summer I was able to spend more time with you after giving up my full-time job at Leeds University in favour of part-time consultancy work. Sometimes I would pick you up to go for a walk on Burbage Rocks or for lunch in the Peak District, at other times give you a lift to Richard G's .He was a former school-friend who also suffered from poor mental health. He was on medication for depression, so not such a serious condition as yours, but we thought you probably had much in common and could offer mutual support. As ever, you still came home to us regularly for a good Sunday lunch and to watch Liverpool FC on TV. And during those months we would occasionally have earnest conversations in which you would try to talk to me about your voices. We would be having a coffee in the conservatory, and it would go something like this:

"Mum, do you think people can actually read your mind?"

"No, Alex, they can't. It may seem like they do sometimes, but they are really just guessing, based on previous experience, and sometimes they can be right. Occasionally I think I know what Dad is thinking because we've lived together for so long and I know him so well."

"OK, but can they put thoughts INTO your mind – things they want you to think?"

"Conversation with anyone can introduce to you new ideas – or reading or watching films and TV. But they can't MAKE you think certain thoughts, Alex – what you make of what you hear or see is completely up to you. Sometimes I can tell when you are hearing voices in your head, but when they tell you things you don't have to agree with what they are saying, do you? And they aren't real. I can't hear them – they are just a symptom of your illness."

We never really got any further than that because you realised I could not fully relate to your voices, and I knew that that is what you were thinking.

On other occasions, I would start the discussion, after noticing that I was losing your attention in some everyday conversation:

"Alex, what are you laughing at? You're not listening to me but to those voices of yours. Why don't you ignore them, tell them to go away?" What are they saying to you?"

But you would never answer that. It was so difficult to know how to allay your fears and fight the very real experiences you were having, even though we could see how devastating they were. It's hard to describe how agonising these exchanges were, how utterly ill-equipped we were to help protect you from them, or at least help you deal with them. But this was a six-month period of relative stability for you, and we began to feel that there was some hope for your recovering a more normal lifestyle. However, another crisis was soon to emerge.

One morning we had a call from your key worker who had arrived at the house to find you not answering the door to your room, but with music emanating from it, indicating that you were present. He found you unconscious on the floor and had called an ambulance. He was now at the Northern General, where they surmised that you had stopped taking your medication, and stockpiled it, including strong tranquiliser/sleeping tablets, to overdose. I spent what would be my third of many more days in future, sitting by your bedside while they brought you round to consciousness and kept you under observation. Your liver was getting used to over-work. I became more blasé about you being in hospital. You, however, always resented being kept in hospital, and spent my whole time with you that day saying you would discharge yourself. I managed to persuade you against walking out, but when I arrived home twenty minutes later, I found Dad had received a call from the hospital saying that you had disappeared. An hour later you were back with us – with a cannula still in your arm! This show of defiance was to be a singular hallmark of your response to your condition – a determination to pretend that all was well really, and that you were in control of your own destiny.

But actually you weren't … As so often, this incident was a precursor to another lengthy spell in hospital – this time Lancaster Ward in the Northern General, as the Michael Carlisle Centre had no beds. The wards in the Northern General were even more soulless than those in the local centre, and also larger, so they seemed more impersonal, and there seemed to be fewer activities organised, not that you availed yourself much of those on offer at Michael Carlisle.
"Alex, why don't you go to the weekly art group?" I had asked in your last stay on Chester Ward, as you had been good at art at school.

"Mum – they just have you colouring in pictures – that is NOT art!" I thought that seemed unlikely, but could not find a suitable response.

"Why don't you go to the weekly gym session – you used to go regularly when you were at university?"

"I went once, but I felt self-conscious… didn't like it."

I didn't ask, but I knew why you had felt self-conscious. For over a year now you had been putting on weight, and it was causing you concern, having been so fit and trim before. This was just one of the side effects of the anti-psychotic medication you had been prescribed, and part of the reason for your resistance to taking it regularly. And the issue of medication side effects was about to become even more significant and worrying in relation to your treatment regime. In another case conference, the psychiatrist explained to us all that the team were concerned about the low level of success they had had with the various medication they had prescribed to date. While your continuous non-compliance was probably the greatest problem – taking it only until you felt better, then stopping – they thought that there was some underlying physical resistance to the treatments they had so far prescribed. They suggested that we should try the strongest possible drug available – Clozapine.

Initially you had been taking Risperidone, with which you experienced no obvious side effects. But it did not seem to be strong enough to deal with the strength of your psychotic episodes, and so you were prescribed first Olanzapine and then later Aripiprazole. With each of these there had been evident side effects. Both occasionally caused you to be restless – when you were standing you would not be completely still – you had to shift your weight from one foot to another. I had noticed this trait in several other patients when visiting you in hospital, so it must have been a fairly widespread effect. There was also one occasion about a year before when you rang me from your flat to say you didn't feel well, and when I drove over, I was alarmed to see your muscles were contracting causing you to bend in on yourself. I took you to the walk-in centre, where you were visibly curling up on the chair, in pain. The staff there could not work out why this had happened, but gave you muscle relaxants, which took effect very quickly, and this problem did not recur. But you rarely had a full night of sleep, and we never knew whether this was a direct result of your illness or a side effect of the drugs. And then there was the significant weight gain, which concerned Dad and I as well as you – since not only did we have a different Alex, personality-wise, than we had known for twenty years, your physical appearance was also changing – it seemed like you were becoming a different person altogether.

And now the team were suggesting you start with Clozapine – the strongest drug available for your condition. We had had a discussion before about starting on this, and you had dismissed the idea, understandably, given the 'health warning' in relation to its side effects. Common side effects of Aripiprazole are listed as:

- weight gain

- blurred vision

- nausea, vomiting, changes in appetite, constipation

- drooling

- headache, dizziness, drowsiness, feeling tired

- anxiety, feeling restless

- sleep problems, insomnia

- cold symptoms such as stuffy nose, sneezing, sore throat.

For Clozapine, to these you need to add 'fast heart rate and increased sweating'. This last item was scarily significant. The staff had explained last time that because of this, you had to start with this drug under observation in hospital for the first two weeks so that they could give you regular blood pressure tests to ensure that you could cope physically with the heart rate acceleration. Even worse, they did warn that there was a strong chance that taking this drug for a prolonged period could mean that you would be prone to strokes at an early age. Such was the seriousness of all this that NICE (National Institute for Clinical Excellence) guidance was that Clozapine should only be prescribed after attempts of using all other alternatives had proved ineffective. How could we encourage you to go for this, however much they said it was your best – perhaps only – chance of seeing any real relief from your psychotic episodes?

If you were not prepared to accept Clozapine, they recommended that you continue with Aripiprizole administered in 'depot' form. They explained this is where they would give you an injection of the drug each fortnight, which would distribute itself evenly over the period. Obviously this would mean that you never missed a dose, and so continued efficacy could be guaranteed. But, of course, this would give you absolutely no control over affairs, and so we were not surprised when you declined this proposal, and agreed to try the Clozapine instead. A bed had become available at the Michael Carlisle Centre, and so you were transferred there for administration of the new drug. Two weeks later you emerged from Chester Ward, having come through a short spell of worrying tachycardia (unduly high heart rate), which settled down after a few days.

Sarah and the team were unanimous in believing that you would not be safe anymore except in a 24-hour staffed environment – but – there was no place available in Sheffield. You had been on the waiting list for Beaumont Road for several months, with no result, so Sarah was going to make further enquiries. Meanwhile, you were home again with us, and we set about, over the Christmas period, trying to encourage you to stick with the new medication to feel the benefits. In those early weeks, we made sure that you took your medication regularly, and we all definitely saw the results. You were much calmer, and we made plans to have a change of scene for Christmas, staying at our cottage in Grange-over-Sands.

The plan was that you and I would drive up on Christmas Eve, bearing all the Christmas supplies, and Dad would bring Matthew up on Christmas morning, once he had enjoyed his annual reunion with old school-friends in Sheffield the previous evening. The day before our travel there was heavy snow, and, although the roads were free the next day, our house-drive in Grange was full of snow when we arrived. Once we had unpacked and had some supper, I thought we should clear the long drive ready for Dad and Matthew's arrival the next day. I remember now, you were sitting in the porch, having a cigarette, when I emerged from the garage with the spade and shovel, encouraging you to work alongside me. You started to help, but were very quickly out of breath, and we laughed when you sat down, announcing that it was probably best if I continue alone.

"You're doing a great job, Mum. I think I'm best at giving the orders!"

Yes, we laughed, but I knew that you were appalled at how unfit you were at the age of twenty-seven, and you probably knew that I was worried about that. Nevertheless we enjoyed the next hour or so, continuing the banter until my job was finished, and then were completely surprised by an unannounced visit from Kathleen and Andrew (Dad's sister and brother-in-law, who were staying with his parents in Grange for Christmas).

I was really pleased at this, since for a year or two now you had shunned any contact with our family members or friends other than Gran, feeling unwilling – probably unable? – to socialise normally. But they had taken you by surprise, and – guess what? – we had a few beers and an hour or so of pleasant light-hearted conversation. They did really well in relating to you exactly as they always had, and you responded equally well. I think we both went to bed that night feeling reasonably happy and hopeful of an enjoyable Christmas. And indeed it was. You turned down the offer of a walk around Tarn Howes on Boxing Day morning with the rest of us, but so too did Matthew as he had a heavy cold, and so you two had some agreeable time together in our absence. We started the New Year with some hope that the new medication might offer the prospect of some recovery for you.

As usual, we were pleased to have you at home where we could supervise your medication, but you were getting restless, wishing to have your own place again. Sarah told us that she was on your case, trying to get a 24-hour supported tenancy for you, but it was proving difficult – there were very few units in Sheffield, and neither you nor we wished to entertain you moving elsewhere. Eventually, however, she rang to say that a place was to become available in March. It was not in Beaufort Road – the 'ideal' supported housing complex in Broomhill – but a project called 911 in Broomhall. It too was managed by South Yorkshire Housing Association, but was not solely for people with mental health issues, but also for those recovering from drug and alcohol problems.

"It's not ideal" said Sarah, "As there is some danger in being exposed to people with a history of substance abuse. But I've discussed this with Alex and he is confident that he will not be unduly affected by this. There is no short-term prospect of a space at Beaufort Road, and so he would like to give it a try. There is a really positive element in that the staff there will supervise Alex in taking his medication regularly, as they do in hospital."
"But he will stay on the waiting list at Beaufort Road?" I responded.
"Of course. The maximum stay for recovery here is two years, so we will seek to move him to somewhere more appropriate as soon as somewhere becomes available."

We were of course not completely happy with this situation, but when we went to visit the place, it seemed a nice environment, and the staff very attentive – they assured us they would keep you on the right track with your medication. So you moved in in April 2011, and we quickly got to know all the staff there, who were happy to discuss your apparent mood and general behaviour with us, and were responsive to my sharing any concerns with them when I returned you back after home visits. The flat was right on the edge of the city centre, so was convenient for you to get around independently, and you were also able to start quite regular meet-ups in town with Richard J, after he'd finished work. This was really encouraging as he had been your best friend at school, but you had seen little of him since making a mess of his house some years before. Since it was close to Waitrose, where I did my weekly shop, we were also able to have a regular coffee routine afterwards at Costa Coffee in Ecclesall Road.

Working from home part-time by now, I was able to establish regular and more frequent contact with you by text – mostly to agree when to get together for coffee or a walk or to come over and watch the football. This seemed to work well most of the time, and also allowed me to assess when you might be having problems, when everything went quiet. Sometimes you would introduce humour into these communications, which always felt good as prior to your illness this had always been a strength of yours. However, often messages came late at night when you should have been asleep.

24Feb.2011
Me – *Are you coming over for lunch today? Mum*
You- *I shall be going out today, so won't see you till Sunday. Rock on.*
Me – *Are you going to watch L'pool in half an hour on Channel 5? Mum x*
You – *No, I'm going to watch it in the living room.*

18 Mar 2011
You (2.35 am) – *""Doctor, doctor, I can't pronounce my f's, t's and h's" "well you can't say fairer than that"*

19 Mar.2011
Me – *Where do you get them from? I'll pick you up at 12 tomorrow.*
You – *Where do you weigh a whale? Think.*
Me – *I've thought but brain not working well. Matthew's number is 07806 567794*
You – *But of course, my dear, it must be a whale weigh station.... dang funny huh.*

On other occasions, you would mix up mundane requests for me to bring over items with random information queries, I presume just to pass the time:

17 May 2011
You *(7.14 pm) – Can you bring me some hay fever tablets please.*
(7.16 pm) – Could you do me a favour and buy me a broom and dustpan and brush to clean my room with
(9.13 am) – Could you also bring me a tin opener and a cheese grater.
Me *– Hello, this sounds suspiciously like a shopping list – will do! Mum x*
You *– LoL thank you, see you tomorrow.*

18 May 2011
You *(2.07 am) – What does QC stand for? Thought maybe queens council but then it wouldn't fit for a king as it were.*
Me *(7.30 am) – I only know queens council – why on earth were you thinking of that at 2 in the morning?! X*
You *(7.35 am) – When are you coming over with my goodies? Are you sure it's queens council? What happens when a king gets in? Ask Dad or look it up it's important for me to know.*
(8.53 am) – Could you bring a bottle of heartburn liquid too – dad should have one slashed somewhere I think.
(8.56 am) – Could you also bring me a Tupperware container for me to keep my cheese in

And on a day when you must have been particularly bored, while I was up in Grange with Gran:

1 Aug 2011
You *(9.31) – Y do they call the radio wireless? Is it because the sound passes through the air and not a telephone wire?*
Me *– Possibly! Mum x*
You *– Steven Gerard's out for the first month of the season. Did you have a good time in Grange?*
Me *– I'm still with Gran. We're having coffee in Dent, North Yorkshire now. She says Hi, how are you? Have you enrolled on your course?*

You (12.05 pm) – No, I'm going in on Wednesday and I'll address the former question with tired, hot and hungry
(1.37 pm) – How long did it take to drive from Grange to Dent? Isn't that a bit far to go for a coffee?
Me – We're on a round trip for the day – lunch in Clapham now. X
You – While looking at the atlas could u educate me as to why they call the midlands the black country? I wish I was on a road trip, not disgruntled, miserable and listening to the Sex Pistols. What's the nearest town so I can look it up in my expensive atlas?
Me – Skipton, would you like to go on a trip with me sometime?
You – That's where Jean Luc Picard lives! Did Dot used to live in Chorley? Black country? Answers on a stamped addressed envelope. I mean text message please.
Me – No, Lin and first husband did before going to the US. Black country – grime from factories? You need to get out doing stuff as you're clearly bored stiff!
You – I've been out 'doing stuff' today. I went and bought a sandwich and played the guitars, and the Sex Pistols aren't boring, they're thoroughly entertaining, perhaps even more interesting than North Yorkshire coffee shops might be, I venture.
I'm not happy with your answer re the black country either, especially from a geography and town planning enthusiast, the black country is a name for the west country not the north of
England...West Midlands, sorry, so where did Dot live – Crosby?
Me – Bury
You – That's right – can't find it in the atlas though.
Me – It's part of Greater Manchester
You – Not only are you ignorant of geographical nomenclature now you're betraying Liverpool and your identity as a scouser – how can you say those words – shame on you, and capital g as well!

Another, related, aspect of your behaviour had been developing around this time – an absolute fixation with books. From an early age you had always been a regular reader, and in your teens had started making your way through the whole range of classic literature. Once at university your degree in Psychology and Philosophy found you learning about all the great philosophers, and even when you were no longer studying, you continued to extend your reading in this area – a trait that, interestingly, you shared with Matthew. You and he could regularly be heard discussing particularly the ideas of Nietzsche. The early change from Psychology to Economics had stimulated also an interest in a whole array of political theory, which similarly continued after the cessation of your formal study. As a result, your book collection continued to grow fairly fast. However this seemed to be becoming an obsession, as you started ordering expensive sets of educational non-fiction hardback book-sets, such as 'The Ascent of Man', and this crystallised into a really bizarre outcome one morning.

The evening before you were at home with us, using my computer, and had asked if you could use my visa to order a book from Amazon, a fairly regular occurrence. You'd then gone back to your flat. I opened up the computer in my home study the next morning to find six separate acknowledgements from Amazon for orders made. On opening them up it transpired that you had ordered dozens of books with a value of around £750! My shout at this realisation brought Dad on the scene fairly quickly, and he had a better idea than I on how to handle the situation. He managed to cancel quite a lot of them before dispatch, but not all, so over the next week our hallway was the centre of operations for returning many bulky parcels. And though you were apologetic, you found it difficult to explain your actions later that day.

Shortly after your move to 911, Sarah announced that your care should have been transferred to the appropriate Community Mental Health Team (CMHT) ages ago, and she could not put this off anymore as resources in her Early Intervention Team were tighter than ever. So William was introduced to us all as your Community Mental Health Nurse (CMHN) and 'Care Co-ordinator'.

At this point I understood what was meant by the term 'Care Co-ordinator'. My part-time consultancy had freed up some time for me to volunteer as a trustee for Sheffield Mind. I had read about this local outpost of the national charity from my extensive research into the mental health system since the onset of your illness, and thought that such involvement would increase my understanding of the local infrastructure, and perhaps help me to have more effective input to your support. As your Care Co-ordinator, William would be responsible for developing a Care Plan for you.

Over a period of years you had developed a trusting relationship with Sarah, who was in her fifties and could have been your mother. We were worried that you may not take kindly to having someone else foisted on you. William was a lot younger and so the relationship was bound to be different. He was only a few years older than you, but from the outset seemed to gain your respect quite quickly, which was important, since there were many staff we came across in 'the system' with whom you had no confidence, and you often let them know this. He also set out with a similar approach to Sarah, being happy to make himself available to me to talk on the phone whenever I had concerns. More than that, he had just finished training in CBT (Cognitive Behaviour Therapy) and said he was going to try some sessions with you. We had had discussions with Sarah on many occasions about the possibility of your having some kind of counselling or therapy to help your condition, rather than just the medication which you always resented so, essential though it was. She had said, and the psychiatrists involved at various stages had agreed, that such therapies could not help you until the underlying psychosis which prompted the voices was fully controlled by the medication, and this required longer-term compliance from you. However, William believed that you had now reached this stage after several continuous months on Clozapine, and had gained the approval of his team psychiatrist for this action. Progress at last?

"How did it go, Alex?" I asked after your first session.
"It was OK I think", William just asked me questions about things I liked and disliked and after discussing these for a while, he suggested I write down or draw what was going through my mind, and then we discussed that."

"What did you draw?"
"I'll just get it", as you pulled a piece of paper from your bag.
I was completely non-plussed by what you showed me.

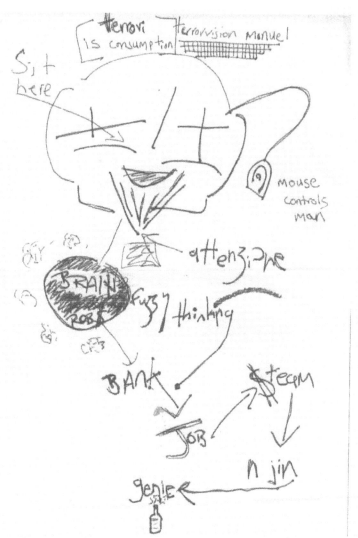

"What does all this mean, Alex?" was all I managed to say.

"These are just the kind of thoughts that go through my head regularly. I'm not going to discuss them again though – it took ages to go through it with William."
"OK, but do you think it will help you?"
"Yeah, maybe, could do. I said I'd carry on with it anyway."
"Good, that's a positive sign." But I have to say I was privately dismayed by what I had seen. How could anyone have such a jumbled set of strange thoughts?
However, you did continue the CBT for another few sessions. Here is another of your drawings from them.

So this seemed a hope for the future, but unfortunately another development was set to sabotage this apparent progress. The Clozapine seemed to have a greater effect on your appetite, so you were becoming seriously overweight, which was causing you distress. And you were also complaining that the drug was dulling your senses to a greater degree than previous medication. You were still walking quite a lot, as you found that therapeutic, helping to clear your head, and also, I would often take you for a walk out on the moors at the weekend, but that was the limit of your exercise, so the weight continued to build...

"What about starting back at the gym, Alex? Or you could get a bike and start using that instead of getting the bus or having lifts from Dad and me? You quite liked cycling across town to the Northern General when you worked there that summer."

"Yes, maybe." I knew that to mean 'probably not'.

However, I persevered with the idea of working more proactively towards recovery, and together we developed a '3-point plan' for how you could re-enter a more normal and healthy life – start studying something, get more exercise, and give up smoking. Things started well. Looking through the Sheffield College prospectus you chose English A level as a test to see if you could develop enough concentration, and you enrolled for September. I explained to your course tutor your illness and she was very understanding saying they could be flexible with the course work when necessary, if you had difficult times. You attended two double lessons a week, and would come back to our house afterwards full of it. The book you were studying first was 'The Kite Runner', which I had read so we were able to discuss aspects of it together. We started walking more regularly, and you did manage to reduce your cigarette consumption.

8. Sectioned and Privatised – September 2011 to

June 2012

Around this time, Matthew was home for a couple of weeks before setting off to start a teaching job in Spain, so we had some nice family time, with various outings and activities. Looking back, though, I might have been concerned, as you became much more animated about everything, because with hindsight I later realised that this was a first sign of your stopping the medication, which, we knew, dulled your senses. You wanted to see the new film 'Tinker Tailor Soldier Spy', so Matthew and I picked you up to go to the Showroom in town. It was apparent immediately that you were far from right, talking very loudly and boisterously. I didn't think sitting in a cinema would be a good idea, so suggested we went for a walk instead, but you wouldn't have it.

"Alex, you can't be like this in the cinema, you know you need to be quiet and watch the film calmly."

"Yes, yes, I know. Don't worry I'm not going to misbehave." Half an hour into the film you said you needed the toilet, and went out, but didn't come back. So I went out to see if I could find you. You were nowhere to be seen, so I had a quick look outside to find you sitting out on the terrace with a beer.

"Alex, I thought you wanted to see this film, so what are you doing out here?"

"It just felt really stuffy in there. I decided I needed some fresh air. That's OK isn't it?" you said in a decidedly belligerent manner that I knew I shouldn't challenge. So I got you to agree to stay there until Matthew and I came out, and then we'd go for something to eat in town.

When we came out, you were on your second pint and talking even louder than before. We sat with you while you finished you beer, but I was beginning to feel really anxious as your voice was getting louder and louder and drawing the attention of passers-by. Eventually we all set off back to the car park, but then you announced that you wanted to spend some time alone with your brother in town, before he went to Spain. I wanted to get you back safely either home or to your flat, but could tell that this was not going to be possible. I was also worried about how Matthew might be in trying to deal alone with your difficult behaviour, in public, having not had to do this before – and whether he would be able to get you back home to safety. There was no way I was going to get you back to the car, so told Matthew quietly I would text him, and left you, returning to the car park decidedly fearful of what might happen. I kept in contact with Matthew by text, simply encouraging him to get you back home or to 911. After about two hours, Matthew arrived home having dropped you off at your flat. He said it had been difficult but that you had started to tire, and so agreed to go home. He had also explained to the staff there that your behaviour had been difficult and erratic, so that they would keep an eye on you.

The next morning we had a call from the 911 staff. There had been a problem overnight with you playing music excessively loud very late, and a Community Mental Health Nurse had been called out to assess your behaviour –¨ William had not been available. You had admitted to her that you had stopped taking your medication and had been stashing them in your room. A further phone call later from Social Services explained that they had suggested to you that you be admitted into hospital, but you were resistant, so they were considering applying a Section to detain you under the Mental Health Act. While I was having this conversation, you rang Matthew saying you were confused and you would like to see him. So Matthew went over. An hour later I was told by Social Services that they would be going to your flat to escort you to hospital early that evening, and they hoped it would be with your acceptance but – given your reluctance up to then – they would have the police with them to effect the hospitalisation under duress if necessary. I agreed with the action since it seemed in your best interests, and explained to them that Matthew was now with you and would be able to encourage you to go to hospital. You did, in the end, go voluntarily; although Matthew, who went with you, reported that they applied the Section and had the police escort you anyway, even though you showed no resistance. He said you were now clearly exhausted but calm.

The next day was Matthew's last before leaving for his new job in Spain so he went to visit you, but you were in very bad humour, as you were with me when I visited you the following day. You were incensed (understandably I thought) that you had been sectioned, and of course with my apparent complicity. The first time you had been sectioned was at the Northern General when Dad and I were in Morocco, and had not been involved, so this marked the beginning of another painful element of your/our situation. Whenever the 'authorities' thought that enforced hospitalisation might be required, and they wanted to apply a Section, part of the procedure was to seek the permission of the 'responsible other adult' in your life. And, yes, that was me – not Dad and me, just me. The law required a single voice in this procedure and specified it should be the elder of the guardians if there were two. So I was starting a journey in which I had regularly to side with the authorities in allowing you to be sectioned, and also sometimes to agree in your appeal process against it to support them again in continuing your hospitalisation. This was to become a regular source of friction between us, although sometimes, I know that you knew I was making the right decision – but I knew that however much you realised that hospital could help, as on several occasions you sought this course of action yourself, you railed against the lack of personal control which the Section process represented. And I understand, Alex, how it must have felt – like being imprisoned for a condition you had no influence over. Of course, I reflected, years ago this would then have been considered a permanent solution to your illness – before the advent of 'community care' – and indeed I had read an account of someone who had been continuously hospitalised in the 1960s. By this time I had read widely of others' experiences with serious mental illness, both from the sufferer's and carer's perspectives and had found some encouragement from several cases where the sufferer had come through with some semblance of normality.

But at the moment, sectioned you were. The next day you were still angry at this, but quite subdued and you became overtly emotional for the first time (in my presence) since

your teenage years, shedding tears on recalling an occasion a week or so earlier, while with your friend Richard G.
"We were listening to some of our favourite music from years ago, and remembering some of the fun times we had camping and things. And it was the first time I really felt happy since I was about eighteen or nineteen" you explained, sitting in the garden of the Michael Carlisle Centre, tears rolling down your cheeks.

This simple statement really hit home and it was all I could do not to cry with you, as I gave you a hug. You had always been the centre of a wide circle of friends, but now...

"Don't worry Alex, we will get you back to that place one day. You just have to persevere with the medication to get yourself on an even keel, and then you can start to re-build your life", I said, feeling anything but confident about this assertion.

"But what about my A level? I'm stuck in here and can't do anything. We're not allowed to have a computer – I asked. I'm not going to be able to finish it."

"Yes you will. The college said they would be flexible with you, so I'll speak to them on Monday and check what you can do. Really, it will be fine Alex, you just get yourself right and ready to start again."

The college did agree you could proceed at whatever pace suited you, and that you should be able to catch up after a spell in hospital since the work you had submitted in the first few weeks had been excellent. I also secured the support of the psychiatrist, Dr Carroll, who agreed you could have leave of absence from Chester Ward between 9am and 5pm to progress your studies. So, during that week, you visited college and our home to organise your work in a different way – you needed to be regularly online to progress successfully. During this time you appeared not at all agitated in conversation, although rather tired, a little distracted, and unable to concentrate to actually do much reading – a consequence, we assumed, of resuming, and getting used to, the medication. I think you must have reached the same conclusion, and so had maybe managed to feign taking your medication (this would take some skill since in hospital the staff supervised this transaction daily), as things started to unravel again.

I was expecting you again the following Friday, en route from college back to the Michael Carlisle Centre, but when you didn't arrive, and didn't answer your phone, I rang the ward. They said you had returned there direct, and someone would ring me back. The Deputy Ward Manager did so at around 6pm, saying that you had provoked an incident in the ward and so they were going to transfer you to a semi-secure unit – near Bradford – since there were no appropriate beds available in Sheffield. I immediately went in to discuss the situation, and was told that you had been making provocative comments around the ward to the extent that one of the patients had been moved to hit you. I asked to speak with you but was told they could not risk this as you were in such a state and it would be dangerous. I responded that that was ridiculous – however agitated you had been hitherto, you had never shown any physical aggression towards anyone, let alone to me. However they were adamant, and the thought of you being taken to Bradford without our speaking with you distressed me, and I arrived home in tears. I returned with Dad, who insisted, successfully, that we were allowed to see you. You were in an isolation room awaiting the taxi to take you to Bradford.

We could quite believe that you had goaded someone into aggression towards you, as you had been known to do this before but, by the time we saw you, you were completely calm, but had several cuts on your face, and were really angry about the situation.
"What's going on, Dad, they're TRANSPORTING me away to PRISON when it was the other guy who hit me?! How can that be right?"
"No it doesn't seem right, Alex, but what did you do or say to get him so annoyed?" Dad replied.
"Well he's got terrible political views – he's racist – and is always spouting about them, so I could not resist challenging him."
"Yes, but if he's not well, and you know how provocative you can be sometimes, perhaps having this approach in the hospital ward is not such a good idea?"
"OK, but still, they can't send me to Bradford, can they?
Dad discussed at length with the Deputy Ward Manager that sending you to a semi-secure unit out of town would do

more harm than good. While we understood his concern about dealing safely with the after-effects of the incident with the reduced night staff, Dad said we could take you home for the night and bring you back in the morning for any new assessments and medication. But Josh maintained that this could not be allowed, since having made the formal referral to a private out-of-town hospital, this could not be revoked, and the staff in Bradford were expecting him. As you would expect, Dad became angry at this point.

"You mean to say that you are prepared to pay for transporting him fifty miles, and for whatever fees are due to the private hospital, when we could take him home quite safely?!"

"Mr Holt, I have taken the action that I deem necessary. If you ring the ward tomorrow they can give you contact details for the hospital in Bradford, and you can make arrangements to visit him there." I still find it hard to believe that the manager was unable to review his decision in the light of new circumstances – how was this reasonable?

So, Sunday morning found Dad and I setting off up the M1 for Bradford, for what was to be the first of several future out-of-town trips to visit you. It was also to be the longest hospital stay you had had yet. We had no idea what we would find at the Bradford hospital, having never been inside a private mental health hospital before. In fact, it was a large converted old mansion house in pleasant grounds in the countryside on the outskirts of Bradford, and inside it looked significantly smarter and brighter than anything at either Michael Carlisle or the Northern General. However, its semi-secure status meant that when we were shown to a room to meet with you, we had to be accompanied by a member of staff, who remained seated at the end of the room, trying to look disinterested in what we were saying. This obviously made it difficult for us to have a frank conversation of how you were finding things there. But in spite of this you were typically blunt when we asked.

"Well it's not that bad I suppose – for a PRISON", shouting the last word, "At least the food's good, and I get to play football. But I don't want to be here – what do I care about BRADFORD?!", again with emphasis.

"I know, we're not enamoured with having to travel so far to see you, but we will come every other day, Alex, and also keep pressure on the Team to find you a bed back in Sheffield" I responded.

"The Team, oh yes the TEAM. Don't expect much luck there then!"

We did have a conversation with a staff member afterwards about what kind of activities there were, and he explained there were art sessions and a reading group, in addition to the regular football sessions, but no, they were not allowed to use computers, as this could not be adequately supervised. So your studies were again going to be on hold.

I spoke to William on the Monday morning, who promised they would transfer you back as soon as anything became available – it was in their interests to do so, since out-of-town accommodation fees were hugely expensive. But I rang again each day to make sure they were continually on your case. We visited three further times that week – Tuesday, Thursday and Saturday, and had occasion for great concern in relation to two of these visits. We arrived on Tuesday afternoon, to find part of the grounds cordoned off with blue and white tape and two police cars parked outside the front door. We enquired what was happening and were told there was a routine security procedure in motion, nothing to worry about. We thought this seemed a bit extreme as a possibility, and so it proved. Watching 'Look North' that evening – our local BBC news programme – we saw a picture of the grounds there, from where a suicide was reported. A 22-year-old young male patient had been found that morning, hanging from a tree in the grounds!! We heard that he had become seriously distressed from being transported away from his home area, somewhere in Cheshire, and had been unable to see much of his parents. And people could be surprised at this? What surprised – and more importantly concerned – us more, was how on earth a patient managed to kill himself in what were fairly limited grounds of a so-called semi-secure unit?

Our fears about this place were further exacerbated at our visit the following Saturday, when we found you had a bruised face from being punched while playing football. And then we had a phone call from you the next day, distressed about being hit again.

So, first thing Monday I was on the phone, insisting to William that if there was no bed available in Sheffield, we wanted you discharged from Bradford, back to our guardianship, to prevent you coming to further harm. But of course William explained that he had no power to do this as you had been sectioned, and your discharge could only be sanctioned by the supervising psychiatrist – who now was one whom we had not ever met – in Bradford. Or or a legal tribunal appeal hearing. Following an inconclusive conversation with the consultant psychiatrist there, I sent the following letter to the manager of the institution:

9th October 2011

Dear Mr Giles

Re. Alex Holt

Further to recent conversations with your Doctor Menzes and staff at the Michael Carlisle Centre in Sheffield, I write to ask formally that Alex be discharged from Bradford, as I do not think he needs to be there and I believe it is actually doing him harm.
When we saw him on Saturday he had a bruised face from being punched while playing football – because a ball he had kicked hit another's chest. There was also another incidence of being punched. He rang yesterday very distressed because he had lent his i-pod to a friend (Hugo), who then claimed to have lost it. Both I and later my husband spoke to staff about trying to find it, and my husband was told they would do so immediately, but Alex rang again to say nothing had happened. We are hoping that when we visit tomorrow, the situation might have been resolved.
Please would you confirm receipt of this letter.

Yours sincerely,
Gill Holt

Unfortunately, of course, no-one was willing to free you from the Section imposed, without the due tribunal process. The Bradford psychiatrist said he had insufficient knowledge of your history to make such a recommendation, and your psychiatrist back in Sheffield said you needed to be back with them for him to be able to make a decision. So – great – nothing would be progressed while you were at Bradford, and it was just a holding operation (literally) until a bed was free in Sheffield, and this took another two weeks. This was a regularly dispiriting factor of your care programme – there was no continuity of care in which you would have an allocated psychiatrist who would take overall charge, irrespective of the hospital ward, obviously in communication with their counterpart. Instead, the psychiatrist in Bradford temporarily took over from the local Team psychiatrist in Sheffield, but seemed to have to 'learn' your story over again.

While we were travelling up and down the M1 you were busy setting in motion the appeal process against the Section, to which you were entitled. You kept us informed, at our visits, about the solicitor who was representing you, and that there would be a hearing of all interested parties in the next few weeks. Meanwhile, we heard that a bed was now available in Sheffield – at the Intensive Service (ITS) Ward at the Northern General. This was, for mental health, the equivalent of the Intensive Care Unit for physical conditions – supposedly offering the highest level of treatment. We were told that now you were back in Sheffield a reappraisal of your situation could be undertaken – your stay in Bradford for nearly three weeks had achieved nothing other than to keep you on the medication – there had been no progress towards your recovery.

After you had been under their observation for a few days – obviously different staff than in Bradford or Michael Carlisle, so they needed to get to know you and how you were presenting and behaving – we were told we would be invited to a case conference to discuss what would happen next. I was not unduly perturbed by this prospect, having already experienced a few at Michael Carlisle. However, even I was slightly overawed by the number of people in the room at the ITS on this occasion. It was a large room with a conference-style table and chairs, and around fourteen or fifteen people spaced around it, two of whom were you and me, sitting next to each other, but I had never met any of them before, other than your CMHN William, and neither had you, before entering ITS a few days before. The woman at the head of table introduced herself as the consultant psychiatrist, before everyone else introduced themselves. She then explained the purpose of the meeting was to decide the best course of action for your future well-being, and invited me to start by saying what I thought of your current situation. I explained how unhappy I was about the preceding incidents that had brought you to their unit, and that I hoped this meeting would at last set you on course for a meaningful journey to recovery. She then asked for your thoughts, Alex, and I was not prepared for your answer.

"Well, take no notice of what she says because she's a waste of space. And I think this whole thing is a massive waste of time. I don't need to be here" you spat out, and then sat back smugly, seemingly pleased with yourself.

It required a great effort not to burst into tears in front of all these strangers, humiliated and, more importantly, hurt as I felt by your words – but I did. And, give her her due, the psychiatrist recognised this and intervened with a suitable comment and moved the agenda forward. They discussed the various options on medication etc, including the possibility of you having the 'depot' approach to medication we had previously discussed, and then, for the first time, the idea of 'rehabilitation' was introduced. This was a new concept to us, but seemed to be a place where patients could go on a fairly long-term basis to have really intensive therapy, away from normal society, and with a high staff ratio input, much like the rehab units we had heard about in relation to drug addiction. After discussion she announced that she would consider everyone's input and then have a one-to-one discussion with you before making a decision on the best way forward. I was quite impressed with the way she handled the discussion, and felt slightly more confident that maybe with her we had found someone more attuned to your needs.

The next day she rang us at home and Dad took the call. "I think we're in luck here" he said, "this woman seems to understand Alex."
"What do you mean?" I replied.

"Well, she had a long one-to-one with him and deduced that he was not going to be satisfied, as many schizophrenia sufferers were, with strong medication to manage his symptoms, and the accompanying limitations to his intellectual capacity, and future prospects. She realised that he still wants to realise the ambitions he had as a teenager – he still feels he can 'go places', do something significant."

"So, does she have a solution to this?"

"No, she is going to make a recommendation that he is found a space in a rehab unit – where he can get the most intensive possible therapy and support to re-find old life skills, underpinned by guaranteed continuity of medication, over a prolonged period of time. And in discussing this option with him, she asked if he would be up for committing to this, to which he replied that no, he would discharge himself at the earliest opportunity, as he could sort out his own problems. So she had told him that she would recommend that he be allocated a place, but that it could be in a locked unit, so that he would have no option of discharging himself. "

"OK, he won't thank us for that of course – but how much weight would this 'recommendation' carry with those holding the purse?", I asked.

"We'll have to see."

This discussion, and my growing knowledge of the mental health scene in Sheffield, prompted me to have a phone discussion with William, enquiring why you did not seem to have a Care Plan, and an associated personal budget – a new idea just being introduced nationally at that time. This was where the patient would work with the Care Co-ordinator to produce a Care Plan suited to their needs, and would be allocated a budget, appropriate to their level of need, with which they could purchase elements of social care suited to their wishes. William explained that you did have a Care Plan but he had not set up a personal budget yet as it was a gradual introduction process in which they were giving priority to those who were less seriously ill, to check how well it might work.

Two weeks later, you were transferred to Michael Carlisle, so it was back to 'business as usual'. An early phone conversation with William revealed that we still had not heard whether you were going to be allocated your rehab space. Meanwhile, your Section Appeal process had progressed, and a hearing was due to take place at Michael Carlisle. As your 'responsible other adult' I was invited and wasn't sure what to expect. It was quite a formal, semi-judicial affair, in which there was an adjudicator flanked by two other panel members, and you were accompanied by the solicitor you were entitled to for representation. The adjudicator asked him first if he was going to speak for you when the time came, but he replied that you would make your own case. So he started the process by asking for evidence from William and the Team psychiatrist on your condition and whether they thought it was appropriate for you to be discharged. Their view was that you had not yet settled satisfactorily back into your medication regime, and required another week or two for this to be achieved. A staff member from 911 had also been invited and they concurred with the Team's view, since they were no longer able to administer medication, following a difficult incident recently, so wanted to be sure you were back in a routine. Then my opinion was sought. I explained that in my view there had been no need for you to be sectioned at the outset, as Matthew had told me you had not resisted being taken into hospital. Also that the situation had been exacerbated – again unnecessarily – by your being transferred overnight to Bradford, adding to the distress all round. However, if the Team's view was that it would take another week or two to for you to return to stability, I would not wish to suggest that you be discharged immediately. I asked if it was possible for the Hearing to express a view on the timing when it gave its view, and was given a positive response. Then it was your turn to express your views. You were surprisingly calm and lucid, and complained, as I had, about what you deemed to be disproportionate responses to your bouts of supposed misbehaviour. However, you did not feel able to agree to the continuation of your hospitalisation. The adjudicator then summed up what had transpired and informed us that he would give the panel's verdict by the end of the day. Before we left he made a point of thanking me for my attendance and input, saying that so often people in your situation had no-one close to them for support and had to go through this alone. I had already been thinking this during the proceedings – remembering all those lost souls in various wards who never seemed to have any visitors, and how daunting it would be for them to experience this process on their own.

As expected, the verdict favoured the Team, and you took the news reasonably well – once your condition was stabilised with continued medication, you were often remarkably stoical about your situation. By this time it was early December and the Team had agreed that you could start a transition process, through which you would start to spend increasing amounts of time with us at home, and then back at your flat. We hoped that that would facilitate the possibility of enjoying a pleasant family Christmas, and then perhaps a move to the recommended rehab unit for the answer to our prayers. In fact, we had a subdued Christmas, and disappointment in relation to the rehab plan – we were told we would not hear anything until the New Year.

On a Saturday about ten days before Christmas, I had arranged to pick you up from your flat to go for a walk and out for lunch, and you were going to stay at ours till Sunday, when I would take you back to Michael Carlisle. However Dad received a call mid-morning from Barrow in Furness hospital – Gran had been taken in overnight with an aneurysm, and was refusing surgery as she had always had a 'Living Will', through which no intervention should be allowed to prolong her life. I rang you to explain we couldn't meet and Dad and I drove up to Barrow. Gran seemed fairly perky when we arrived, but we were told that she had been given morphine to reduce the pain she had been feeling. We had a discussion with the staff, confirming that her Living Will requirements should be honoured, and so it would be just a matter of time for the bleeding to take its toll. During the day, the rest of her family arrived from further afield, and we took our leave early evening, needing to get back to Sheffield to keep an eye on you. We received a call, en route, from Dad's sister Ainslie to let us know that she had died.

Again there was almost – but not quite – a tear or two from you when I told you of Gran's demise. Gran had nine grandchildren from her four children and she loved, and had been hands on, with all of them. But certainly, it seemed, you and she had had a particularly good relationship. I worked it out that in the twenty nine years since the last Christmas we had celebrated Christmas at her house in Grange when you were a baby, she had spent all but two with our family in Birkenhead, Grange or Sheffield. In spite of your illness I think you realised, as the rest of us did, how much we were going to miss her, particularly at Christmas, which was almost upon us. Matthew was working in Spain, and not able to return home until Christmas Eve, so we decided it was best to save telling him about Gran until he returned home. He arrived from Seville to John Lennon airport on Christmas Eve morning, and I told him what had happened with Gran. Obviously he was devastated by the news, and cried on and off all the way back to Sheffield – Gran had been a major factor in all our lives for many years, since the much earlier demise of the other three grandparents.

So, we had the prospect of a Christmas without Gran, and one that was overshadowed by Dad making arrangements for her funeral in the New Year, and me thinking of the tribute to her that I had been asked to make at it. However, actually, the situation seemed to bring us together, and we did manage to have a pleasant, if a little subdued, Christmas. There was another factor also operating over this period – Matthew had given notice for his job in Spain (as it wasn't turning out as good as might have been) and had a Skype interview lined up with a teaching agency about a job prospect in Taiwan, which was eventually fixed on the date of Gran's funeral, when we would all (but not you of course – you could not cope with the socialising involved) – be up in Grange. So, one day in early January saw Dad, Matthew and I travelling up to Grange ready for the funeral the following day. It went as smoothly as these things can, and Matthew had his Skype interview, which succeeded in securing him a year's contract teaching English as a second language in Taiwan. Two weeks later, we saw Matthew off on the train to London en route to Tapei – and so we were now down to three – just you, me and Dad.

But by then, you seemed to us much more relaxed and content, so we assumed you were taking your medications regularly, and life resumed its former pattern. We had liaised with the staff at Sheffield College, and you resumed your A level English. It didn't take you long to complete, successfully, the work from the previous term, but I was slightly perturbed when I learned that for term two you would be studying 'Cat on a Hot Tin Roof' – focussing on the mental illness of a central character.

Because of your A level you had been using my laptop a lot at this time, and one day I found a long list of saved files. Curious, I opened them up to find about twelve or thirteen poems, which I could tell from the 'saved' dates, had been created over the space of four or five days. They were amazing Alex. I have never been hugely interested, and certainly not knowledgeable, in poetry, but I could tell there was definite merit in these. Some had decidedly unusual content and/or language, but mostly I found them pleasantly intriguing. There was one particularly touching one – a love poem, which seemed to be addressing someone specific in your life and I wondered who it might be. Caroline perhaps? I printed them off, and when you next came round, waved them at you, suggesting that you share them with your tutor at college to see what they thought of them. Seeing them had given me the idea that you might have a future in the literary world, something that may be more possible than other occupations, not necessarily requiring significant socialising skills.
However, a few days later I asked you about this, and you replied, scoffing:
"No, I didn't show her – no-one would be interested in my ramblings!"
"But Alex, I think they would. I found them really moving."
"It's too late now anyway, cos I've got rid of them."
"Well, I'll keep them for myself."
"No you won't – I've deleted the files."

I was so disappointed, but this reminded me of a similar situation some years ago. The morning after your return to Sheffield in 2006, the day you tried to take your life, I had found you scribbling among sheafs of paper. When I asked what you were doing you distracted me into making breakfast. However, the next day, while you were in hospital, I had looked at these, to find you were in the process, incomplete, of writing a letter to me – what was, in fact, a suicide note. You had started to explain about how you had struggled with various issues over the years, and, completely overwhelmed, I put it to one side to discuss with you later, if we could. However, I had left the papers in a file on the coffee table, and on your return from hospital you managed to destroy them before I had a chance to discuss them with you.

In relation to your poems, though, shortly after you had deleted the first tranche, I noticed another list of saved files growing and quietly printed them out as they materialised. Again they were all produced within a single week, but they were generally much darker in content, and more shocking in the language and phrases used. But they seemed to constitute a sharp, sometimes cynical and sometimes savage, reflection on a range of your experiences through this awful illness. Here are some examples:

Bedtime
I love my bed, let it be said,
That it erodes the anger buzzing round my head
A safer place I'll never find,
To soothe my soul and ease my mind.
The pillow obliges my need for support
As my brain dissolves superfluous thoughts.
I'll slip away into the night
My conscious turns off in synch with the light.
Then I'm gone, but how will I return?
Will I have learned not to speak out of turn?
Certainly this mystery,
Tells what my bed means to me,
As I've had to at times sleep on empty park benches
I now give my bed undivided attention.
The last time my bed indulges my sleepy eyes

Will be my denouement, or the day that I died.

Dear Ma

Ma, Dear Ma, I'm jaded and lost,
I knew I was a cynic, but did not know the cost!
I knew not the value of all manner of things,
So hard to fly when they've broken your wings.
But Ma, Dear Ma, I'm planning my escape
Signing terms and conditions to break through red tape.
Though always alone, somewhat accident prone
Living in glass houses, and inclined to throw stones.
I'm fighting the ghoulies, lest they run amok.
My days aren't yet numbered, but tik-tok, tik-tok.
I saw what I thought was a distant mirage,
Looking all silly, thinking it a macabre farce.
On closer inspection the nuances grew,
Informing me of all the habits to eschew.
At times when I'm alone, I've let out a groan,
And dreamed of Dear Ma and a place once called home.

Hospital bed

Lying in a hospital bed
Regret and fear devouring my head
I tried to remember whilst hoping to forget
My lost identity peering over the parapet
The rusty razor had left me supine
From hallucinations that had seemed divine
Psychotic desperation had carved out tattoos
A Memento Mori, though a little bit crude.

A girl by my side merged with one in my head
Escorted me away from pangs of sheer dread
She whispered sweet nothings, then we followed trombones
We wandered through forests collecting pine cones
Then came the trumpets announcing escape
Death had been thwarted but I was in bad shape
Finally the slow narcotic jazz sax
We held hands as it faded, then I detached.

I woke from my slumber
My wrists were encumbered
With bondage and drips

That were giving me gip
As was the hum of surrounding machines
They're always so humdrum these hospital routines.

Though grateful euphoria rattled through my bones
Confusion returned knocking as I watched the nurse clones
They all looked so pretty yet apposite aloof
Guess they've seen plenty and can handle the truth.

Wetherspoons and Night Time
We sat in Wetherspoons pub, a veiled hall of mirrors
Faces clearly reflecting my existential shivers
Was it me, was it them?
Was it all of us gaggled in like an opium den?

A place for regret, but we'd come to escape
Now I was feeling like my perception had been raped
We left in a hurry
A fidgety scurry
Headfirst into the bookmakers – double 8 8.

Why run in here? We laughed with a sneer
If before we were worried, it was now more severe
From the proverbial Frying Pan to the Moribund fire
The place full of spendthrifts, we wanted the high wire!
We wanted to gamble with life not with money
We wanted epiphany while crapping on a dunny!
We needed to return to bestial highs
Ones built for shame inculcated to despise.

We needed the circus in all its ironic pomp
So anyhow we went to the cinema for a celluloid romp
We stay through a saccharine song and dance movie
Pathetically uplifted, thinking it burlesque and groovy

After our day in the centre of town
No closer to lifting our pathetic frowns
We'd come for a break
It was such a mistake
And so we toddled home feeling downer than down.

We rested with a snooze, now with nothing to lose
We headed for bright llights,
The catalyst – booze.

Night time
Night time
Definitely the right time
Night time
Night time
Taciturn delight time.

Our freewheeling fancy led us straight to the club
We'd not been for ages but heard it was a hub
For liars and drifters and will 0 the wisps
The type who hold steadfast when faced with cease and
desist
Though we laughed at the bouncers and their mindless
charade
And their obtuse demeanour as they herd in the cavalcade

William had decided, following your previous difficult period, that CBT was not an option again for a while, and so it was back to the 'medication only' model of treatment. And we were, at last, informed, on asking, that the recommendation for secure rehab had been turned down. The Team did not seem to know on what grounds it had been turned down, but we all assumed it was a decision based on finance – they were not prepared to pay. It seems the only place that was available was in Newcastle, and buying in this space would probably have been a huge cost on the Sheffield NHS budget. We later found out, through a formal serious incident report produced by the Care Trust, that in fact the NHS panel who considered the consultant's recommendation of locked rehab, decided to disagree, saying that locked rehab 'wasn't necessary' - on what evidence we do not know. You were not concerned at this as you had never bought into the idea of locked rehab, but Dad and I then believed that this might be your 'last chance saloon', and so it was a real blow. But we steeled ourselves for more 'business as usual'.

There was another occasion in the first few months of 2012 when you stopped taking medication again, and consequently there was another short spell in Chester Ward. As often was the case, after you had been discharged from hospital you were assigned the support of the 'Home Treatment Team'. This meant that for a few days after discharge they would visit every morning to check up on your mood and ensure you had taken your medication, and after that would be available, at the end of a phone, for ad hoc support. However, on the only occasion I felt the need to seek this support, I was not impressed with the response.

You rang up one afternoon in late March to ask if we could go for a coffee, so I picked you up from the flat and headed for Costa Coffee in Ecclesall Road. However, you said you wanted to go to Nonna's, the Italian restaurant instead, so we could sit outside on their terrace as it was a warm spring afternoon. We were not long into our coffee before I realised that all was not right with you. Your knee was twitching, you seemed agitated, and you were talking very loudly and slightly aggressively. I drank mine quite quickly, and suggested we go for a walk – an attempt to get you into more controllable territory.
"No, Mum, let's have another drink, it's really nice here", and you disappeared inside to get them.
You reappeared with two cocktails – oh dear, it was only 4.30pm.
"Alex, what on earth have you got these for? It's not a good idea to be drinking cocktails at this time of day – and I'm not keen on them anyway."
"Well I think it's a nice change from Costa, a bit different. I'll have yours if you don't want it."

You then started to chat to anyone sitting near us, and also made comments to passers-by on the pavement. People were looking embarrassed as you persisted in commencing conversations about nothing in particular, and I sensed your annoyance growing when they ignored you.
"Alex, people want to talk to each other, not to you, Come on, if you're bored, let's drink up and go for a walk before tea."
"No, I'd like to stay here for a while – it's great having all these people to speak to."

I was not going to get you away from there anytime soon, and you were becoming increasingly belligerent.

"Alex, you seem quite agitated, I think you should take one of your anti-anxiety tablets." These were prescribed for you to take as and when necessary.

"I haven't got any – they're back at the flat. Anyway I'm OK, I'm enjoying myself."

This was going to be a long afternoon. I went inside the restaurant and asked the barman not to serve you any more alcohol if you asked, as you were ill, and he agreed. I then found the manager and explained to him that you were ill and having a bit of a noisy episode, but that I would try to get you away as soon as possible. But you were insistent on staying, and went into the bar, coming back out complaining that they wouldn't serve you anymore. With no sign of you agreeing to go, and with your agitation levels growing, I rang the Home Treatment Team number,

"Hello, I'm Alex Holt's mum, and am with him at the moment outside Nonna's restaurant, where we came for a coffee and have been for the last hour and a half or so. I'm worried that Alex is becoming increasingly agitated, and bothering passers-by noisily, and I'm worried that we might have some trouble if he doesn't calm down. He refuses to leave, and doesn't have his anti-anxiety tablets with him, so I wonder if you could bring some to us, as they should calm him down, and then I can get him home."

"Well, Mrs Holt, he is an adult, and is perfectly able to decide whether and when he leaves. This isn't the kind of situation in which we would be involved."

"But you don't understand – when he gets like this he can be really belligerent with strangers, and I'm worried that there is going to be trouble. We've been here two hours now and he's just refusing to leave. Without his tablets he's just getting worse."

"I'm sorry, but I'm sure everything will be OK – he'll go home when he's ready. If he does become too aggressive you should call the police." Ah – the police again – last resort! There seemed no prospect of movement on this pronouncement, so that was it – the Home Treatment Team staff member, who had never met you, knew better than I, apparently, what to worry about and what not.

Meanwhile, the manager came outside to see what was going on as you were making quite a noise, making loud unwelcome comments to strangers. The restaurant inside and out was filling up now, with people coming after work as Friday evening progressed. He was very understanding when I told him I was failing in my attempt to get you to leave, but would continue to try. We had some of your tablets at home, but Dad was out of town for the day, so probably not available. But I tried his number anyway – no answer, so I left a voicemail message.

But then – a call out of the blue; the Home Treatment Team must have decided some action was necessary after all: "Hello Mrs Holt, I'm PC Chalmers. We've just received a call from Social Services explaining that you are having a problem with your son at Nonna's and may need help. We are just turning into Ecclesall Road, and will be there in a few minutes, so perhaps we could have a quiet word with you?"
I saw the car turn round the corner at the side of the restaurant, so told you I was going to the toilet, and went to speak with her. She asked did I want them to intervene and force you to go home and I explained that I did not want to over-react – I had managed to keep things controlled up till now, but was worried how much longer I could keep it up. But of course I wanted to avoid you being marched off by the police if possible. So she gave me her number, saying the car was going to be in the vicinity for the next couple of hours, and that I could ring her if an incident was developing and they would come immediately. That was so reassuring – ..to know that if something did happen, help would be at hand quickly.
Shortly after that, Dad rang having picked up my message when he arrived home. He was setting off with your tablets, and suggested that maybe the two of us together might be better able to persuade you to leave. You were happy to take the tablets – we had another coffee each by now – but angry at Dad apparently interfering in our coffee meet, trying to get you to leave, so we agreed that Dad would go home and we would follow when you were ready. Fortunately the tablets took effect fairly quickly, and twenty minutes later I

could tell that you were becoming calmer, quieter, and starting to focus your conversation solely on me again, so I was emboldened to try once more "Shall we go home now Alex – it's time for tea, and you must be hungry?"
"Yes I am hungry – can we eat here Mum?"
As soon as you said that, taking on board the way you said it, I knew we were back 'on solid ground' again, and the prospect of a nice Italian supper was quite attractive...
We emerged from the restaurant, after a pleasant meal, at eight o'clock, nearly five hours after we had arrived! I now had a parking ticket, having overstayed my welcome by about three hours, but did I care...You were exhausted, and so was I, so we both went to bed early. It was hard to believe that two tablets could have such a profound effect on your ability to function normally.

The Nonna's incident had been a temporary blip, and we had a straight run through to your birthday in April. We assumed you had kept to your medication regime and you seemed to be working well on your A level. I asked if you would like to go somewhere special for your birthday, and you chose Chester Zoo. You had always loved animals, and had chosen this destination for your birthday in two separate years, as a young boy. I felt confident enough about your disposition to suggest that we could stay overnight so that we could spend the next day looking round where you had lived as a baby/toddler, and also Liverpool city. You jumped at the idea, so 21st April saw us set off from Sheffield first thing, arriving at the zoo just as it opened at 10 am. How you loved that day. You were absorbed in everything you saw – and we saw everything! You had much to talk about and we had a lovely lunch outside in the spring sunshine. By 4.30pm we were both tired with all that walking and set off to find old haunts on the Wirral. We stopped first at West Kirby, a seaside village on the Dee estuary, where Dad had regularly windsurfed, and where we often went for Sunday walks and lunch when living in Birkenhead. We sat on a bench overlooking the marine lake, while you rolled a cigarette, the sun still shining and warm.
"This is lovely" you announced, "It's just like being on holiday", and I thought yes, it's a long time since you have been any distance from Sheffield for anything pleasant. We

enjoyed the sun for half an hour or so before returning to the car and travelling through Birkenhead, looking at the house you had lived in before moving to Sheffield, and then on via the Mersey Tunnel to the hotel I had booked for overnight. This was a golf resort hotel outside Formby, so not far from where I grew up in north Liverpool. You really enjoyed our evening meal there, and we both agreed that an early night was in order after all that walking, and to meet for breakfast at eight. You said you were going to watch the film on ITV in bed, as a treat. I returned to my room, anxious that you may 'go walkabout' during the night, as you did sometimes at home when you were restless, so I planned to watch the film also and not settle down until I knew you were asleep. I had asked for two keys to your room so that I could reassure myself on this. During the second set of adverts I rang your room to be sure you were still there, and received no answer, so set off down the hall to check. I was still some distance away when I heard it – loud TV emanating from behind your door. I knocked, but no answer, so entered with the key, to find you fast asleep. You had clearly been exhausted by your busy day. I turned off the TV and went to sleep reassured that you were safe for the night.

The next morning I rang again to make sure you were up, and you were, sounding quite perky. You enjoyed the full English breakfast before we set off again in the car. We first drove through Formby to see the neighbourhood where your hero, Steven Gerrard, (captain of Liverpool FC and England) lived, before travelling to Thornton, where I showed you my childhood home. From there we drove straight into the city centre, and you were really interested in wandering around the area where the Cavern was situated. You showed just as much interest in all the statues around the civic quarter, including one of William Gladstone, who came from Liverpool. We then went to the Slavery Museum, where you were appalled at the distressing story displayed there. On the way out, as a sort of postscript, there is a small section on the Toxteth race riots of 1981, and I explained that I had worked in a housing office in Lodge Lane there at that time, to which you replied you wanted to go and see it.

"Well, Alex, I'm not sure I could find it now – the roads will probably all have changed, but I'll try, as it's almost on the way back to the M62", (our route home to Sheffield).
"Oh and I'd like to see the two cathedrals, too, Mum?"
"We won't have time to look around them now, and they won't be open – it's already six o'clock. But they are close together and both more or less on the way out to Toxteth, so we can drive past for you to have a look."
So you saw both cathedrals and also I did find my old office in Lodge Lane, before heading off home, arriving back in Sheffield at around eight thirty. You stayed with us that night and were full of what you had seen, telling Dad all about it.

After you'd gone to bed I spoke with Dad.
"Well that was the best two days I have spent with Alex in about five or six years. He so enjoyed it, and chatted away all the time. If only he can stay like this, he must have a good chance of recovering a reasonable life."
"Yes, I can tell he had a good time – he hasn't been so positive about anything for ages."
So I had no compunction about leaving Dad for ten days while I travelled to Taiwan in May to see Matthew. It was lovely to spend time with him in that unusual and interesting location. Taipei, the capital, was a bit like an oriental Los Angeles. We had some lovely walks around the Toroko Gorge, in the highest range of mountains east of the Himalayas, staying in a hotel that was originally a holiday retreat for Ho Chi Min; and also a couple of days swimming from the beach in a national park just outside Taipei. It was a shame, though, that Dad could not be with us. But it was good to arrive home to find that you were still in a fairly good place, with no untoward behaviour while I was away.

9. New Friends? – July 2012 to January 2013

Our hopes were maintained through the next few months as you continued on a reasonably even keel, although you were spending less time with us, and not answering your phone too promptly. But soon we were to feel the effects of your living in accommodation which also housed ex-substance abusers. Occasional enquiries as to whether a place in Beaufort Road would soon be available for you had been met with negative responses, so you seemed destined to rub shoulders with people experiencing these problems for the foreseeable future.

Then there was a bolt from the blue on the opening Saturday night of the London Olympics in August. I was enjoying the opening ceremony, while Dad was at the gym, when the phone rang.

"Hello. Is that Mrs Holt?"

"Yes", already anxious.

"This is Nurse Edwards from Rotherham General Hospital. I thought you ought to know that we have Alex here. He was brought to us by the police this afternoon, after they had a call from a member of the public saying that they thought his behaviour was unsafe."

"Unsafe – what do you mean?"

"We don't have any more details, but he is perfectly OK and we are arranging for him to stay at a mental health unit close-by for the night, where his exact condition will be assessed." She gave me the contact details and said we could visit him the next day at two o'clock.

What could you possibly have been doing in Rotherham? And what was the nature of your unsafe behaviour? I was impressed, though, that Rotherham General had seemingly handled the situation so well.

On Sunday afternoon, I pulled up outside a lovely new building on the outskirts of Rotherham. Modern, light and airy, this mental health centre could not be more different from those grim down-at-heel buildings with which we had become accustomed in Sheffield. The nurse explained to me what had happened to bring you here. Apparently you had been at a bus stop and had started walking backwards and forwards in the middle of the road, so someone waiting for a bus had rung the police to stop you coming to harm. She said you seemed fairly calm today and they were arranging for you to be transferred to the Michael Carlisle Centre tomorrow. Then she pointed to where you were sitting – in a most delightful garden.

"Hi Alex. What have you been up to this time? What on earth were you doing at a bus stop in Rotherham?" I had never had the need to go to Rotherham, and as far as I knew, neither had you.

"Well, I thought yesterday I'd like to go on a trip so went to the station and bought a ticket to Goole."

"Goole – why Goole? I don't think there's much going on there."

"No – there wasn't! And there weren't many trains back either, so I found a bus, but got off too early, in Rotherham."

"OK, but what made you think walking in the middle of the road was a good idea?"

"I was bored waiting for another bus back to Sheffield, and it was quite safe – there was no traffic around at the time. This bloke kept telling me to stop which annoyed me so I wasn't going to, but then the police turned up."

"Well I hope you're not going to do anything like that again – it's just got you back in hospital."

"No, on reflection, it wasn't my best idea."

That was the thing with you, Alex. So often you would exhibit bizarre behaviour, creating anxiety amongst those around you, but afterwards you could discuss the incident very lucidly in a matter-of-fact way, as though you were analysing the activities of someone else.

You did not remain in hospital on this occasion. Instead, the Team found you a place at Howard Road, a unit which provided respite care, where you would stay for a week or two, with 24-hour support. Unfortunately, this meant that you were unable to enrol for the second year of your A level. Once you were back at your flat at 911, I picked you up from there one morning, to go for a coffee, and you introduced me to 'your new friends'. I had seen the young woman around the flats for some months, but not the young man, who apparently was her boyfriend. At Costa Coffee you explained that Janice was a fellow tenant who was there to recover from a drug addiction, and that her boyfriend Paul lived not far from your flats, across the dual carriageway. In our ensuing conversation I was somewhat alarmed at the significance you were placing on having these new friends, and thought back to conversations Dad and I had had when you first moved in – querying the advisability of mixing those with mental health issues with substance abusers. But you had had no choice – it was there or stay at home with us. Every now and then we asked about where you were on the Beaufort Road waiting list to be told there was no chance of a place in the near future.

For the next few months, there was a build-up of difficult behaviour from you, resulting in a series of worrying incidents. On one occasion, I picked you up from the flat and gave you a lift to the pharmacy which provided you with a monthly programme of medication. This was prescribed in weekly blister packs, labelled for each day, to make it easier to remember all the different tablets, and keep to the regime. When we arrived at Costa Coffee, I asked if you were going to take this morning's tablets.
 "Nope – I don't have them. I threw them straight in a bin by the chemist." You had that cocky, defiant, look which signalled a difficult conversation ahead.
"What?!"
"I'm not taking that stuff anymore, Mum, it makes me feel like shit and it doesn't help. I don't need it."
So I had to get an emergency Saturday morning appointment with your doctor to get a new prescription. She had never met you before and rather brusquely remonstrated with you as to why you thought it acceptable to throw away such expensive medication.
"I'm just fed up with them all. They don't seem to work anyway."
"Well, I've just reviewed your notes, and they show that whenever you stop taking them you become ill again. So how do I know you will take them if I prescribe more?"
"I'll make sure he will" I intervened.

At this time you were also reacting very badly to any reference I made to my work at Sheffield Mind.

"Oh, so Sheffield MIND have the answers to my problems, do they? Yes, Sheffield MIND, Mum, of course – why did I not think of that?" Your pronunciation of MIND was sinister as well as loud.

I assumed you felt that they, too, like your Team, were part of the problem rather than solution, so stopped mentioning it after a while.

Then there was the night that your friend Richard G rang us to say that you had been at his flat all afternoon and had been in a 'weird mood' so he'd asked you to leave but you refused. Again Dad had had to enlist the help of the police in persuading you to leave. I immediately went over to see you and found you were indeed in a 'weird mood', unable to explain why you thought it OK to upset your friend and take advantage of his hospitality. I noticed, however, that Paul was there again, in the living room with Janice. I shared my concerns with the staff, suggesting that you may have been influenced by this couple, and that perhaps you were taking some kind of drug. They had no evidence of this and also explained how they could not stop Janice from having visits from her boyfriend.

However, I was convinced that you were 'on something'. Although you had often had bouts of bizarre, and sometimes aggressive, behaviour, now you seemed to have a different look – what people used to call 'spaced out'. On several occasions when I spoke with you or sent texts, you proudly announced you were with, or going to see, your new friends, now visiting Paul's house in Gell Street. I shared my concerns with William, who agreed that your behaviour had become more unstable again, but that you were adamant you were not taking drugs, and there was no evidence to suggest otherwise. He would try to warn you about getting too involved with Paul, and a wider circle of his friends in Gell Street. This prompted me to ask yet again when you might be allocated a space at the Beaufort Road supported housing scheme, having been on the waiting list for nearly two years, so that we could keep you away from those with a history of substance abuse. He reported back that there was no sign yet of anything becoming available,

These incidents and this behaviour continued, and so I had considerable anxiety about leaving Dad to keep an eye on you alone while I set off in November on another trip to Taiwan, followed by a meet-up with my friend in Australia, followed by a visit with my sister and family in New Zealand – I would be away for nearly a month. However Dad told me not to worry, and that he was quite able to provide any support alone. He did, however, get a little tetchy with me when I would email him most days to ask how you were. "What's the point of that, Gill? You can't do anything about what's going on, so all you're doing is spoiling your holiday, and getting me agitated. Just relax." Fair point, so I tried not to ask after you anymore.

But when I returned home at the end of November, I discovered that there had been a new and serious incident the previous week. You had been with Dad at our house and disappeared – he couldn't find you but knew you hadn't left the house. In the end he found you in the cellar – with a bloody ear; for the first time since you had slit your wrists in 2006, you had self-harmed, cutting behind your ear with a kitchen knife. He had taken you to A and E where they had fixed you up, and William had come to the house to have a joint session with you and Dad. It seemed you had recently stopped taking the medication and they had agreed that while there was no need for you to be hospitalised, the Home Treatment Team would visit with you at your flat each morning for a while to ensure that you were complying with medication. However, Dad and I continued to worry about your connections with the Gell Street people, and your demeanour did not improve much, leading up to Christmas.

And what a bleak Christmas it was. First, there was the reminder that Gran had died just before last Christmas; second, it would be the first one we would spend without Matthew, who was in Taiwan; and also your cat, Squeak, had been diagnosed with 'pull-tail', a condition in which both back legs were paralysed. The vet had advised that sometimes it would right itself, but it was less likely in one of her age – she was, after all, eighteen years old. He urged that the most humane action would be to have her put down after Christmas if the condition continued.

I suggested that you move in to our house a few days before – I wanted to keep you out of harm's way and be sure you were able to join us for the day. But you were adamant that you would spend some more time with your friends, and would not agree even to come round on Christmas Eve. I kept in touch by text, and hoped that you would indeed find your way round to ours when everyone else might also have family commitments, saying that we would pick you up as there would be no buses on Christmas morning. In the event, we had had no communication when I went to church in the morning, nor by the time I had returned. We were just about to set off to pick you up when you arrived, having walked all the way from your flat. There is no way that you had not taken something untoward leading up to that morning. You looked dreadful and not able to communicate very well at all. You managed to eat some of the lunch I had prepared before saying you were tired and taking yourself off to bed. You slept for about seventeen or eighteen hours, with me checking up on you every now and then to be sure that you were just sleeping. What had you been taking? And how could we find out and do something to stop it?

When you re-emerged on Boxing Day morning, you did seem much better, and you brought your tablets down with you, which was at least one good sign. After a late breakfast, Dad suggested that we all go for a walk to get some fresh air, but you asked if you could go on a bike ride instead. We only had two bikes, so you and Dad set off for Derwent Reservoir, with the bikes on the back of the car. Later, our friend Dinah appeared at the door asking if we would like to join them for lunch at the Bull's Head up the road, after their house party had taken a walk in the park. I explained the situation and left a note for Dad to join us if you returned soon enough and he felt able to leave you. This he did about an hour later, reassuring me that you had really enjoyed the ride, and had told him to join us at the pub, as now, quite tired, you would like to watch TV. After several weeks of stress and worry leading up to Christmas and a dismal day itself, it was so nice to have a relaxed time with friends for a few hours, in the knowledge that you were safe, and seemingly quite well, in our house. You stayed with us for most of the time through New Year, very quiet, but seemingly content and so again I was not too worried when I bid you goodbye, as I prepared to set off for a week of tennis at a friend's holiday home in Florida.

But I did feel guilty. This was my third trip in twelve months, while Dad had not been anywhere. Indeed since the doomed Moroccan trip nearly four years earlier, he had had just one weekend in Paris with me, the previous year. This was his choice – I would have been happy for him to have time out somewhere, and had suggested several times that he could go snowboarding, something he had done before on his own – but he insisted he did not need to and there was no need for me to feel guilty about my travels. But I did. However, I enjoyed the tennis and the sun, and returned well rested for whatever was to happen next. Dad had informed me by email that he had had to have Squeak put down, and as a result, when I arranged to have a coffee with you on my return, you were angry, complaining that "Dad has killed the cat." Dad had explained to me that she had kept dragging herself out through the cat-flap to sit in the garden, waiting to be attacked by magpies, clearly thinking her time was up. Dad kept bringing her back in, but eventually had taken her to the vet. I could not understand how you could really believe that it was not necessary to have her put down. Only a young child could take such a view. What had happened to your common sense? But then we were soon to find out just how irrational you could be, with a bizarre incident that set the scene for the most traumatic period of your illness.

One Friday in January you arrived at ours at about 7pm, asking if you could borrow Dad's bike again at the weekend, which of course we agreed to. Half an hour later, you were nowhere to be seen. We noticed the mountain bike was missing from the garage, so you must have gone for a ride – not a good idea on a freezing cold evening, in the dark, in January. Even worse, we found a pile of clothes on the front doorstep – your anorak and jeans. What were you wearing? I rang 911 and asked the staff to let us know if you returned there, but heard nothing. When you hadn't returned by 1.30am, Dad drove to Castleton (your favourite destination for a bike ride, about fifteen miles from home), but did not come across you. I then drove over to your friend Richard

G's house, to see if your bike was outside there but it wasn't, and so, after a few hours of fitful sleep, I rang the police at 8 o'clock to report you missing. Not much more than an hour later they rang back to say that you were in the Northern General, for observation for hyperthermia. It seems that the previous evening a man driving back to Sheffield from Manchester had come across you on the Snake Pass, walking your bike towards Sheffield, and wearing only a sweatshirt and boxer shorts. Not surprisingly, you had been sectioned, and there was the usual assessment process and transfer to Michael Carlisle, before you returned home to us a week later.

Was this bizarre behaviour triggered by drugs? You denied, once again, that your 'new friends' were supplying these to you, and you were still having regular review meetings with your Care Co-ordinator, William, who was pleased that you had been asking about getting some work experience, through a project with a charity which aimed to ease people with difficulties back into work. And your bank account was still in the black, so you hadn't been spending beyond your means. However, even the Snake Pass incident had not prepared us for the disturbing and distressing chain of events which was about to unfold. For perhaps the first time, your demeanour and behaviour would push Dad and I – and indeed now Matthew also – beyond the limits of our capabilities for keeping you safe.

10. A Month in the Life – February to May 2013

The next few weeks I can honestly say that our lives unraveled. Your disturbing and distressing behaviour over this period prompted me to record the chain of events, afterwards, and to produce from it an analysis of where the mental health system in Sheffield was malfunctioning. Someone had to acknowledge where things were going wrong and try to set them right.

On Friday afternoon 1st February, you left our house, supposedly to return to 911, but later, at about 6.30pm, Dad was returning from a bike ride, with the bike in the back of the car, when he saw you walking along the Snake Pass. You told him you were walking to Manchester, no explanation as to why. Although once again it was freezing cold, he could not persuade you to get in the car and come home with him.

"You didn't leave him there?! I shrieked at Dad when he told me this.

"Yes – I had no choice. I tried to push him in, but he's too strong Gill."

"I'm sure you could have persuaded him if you'd tried harder. You can't just let him walk to Manchester in this weather – it's nearly forty miles!" I virtually hissed at him.

"OK – you go and persuade him then, if you think it's so easy. The whole situation is completely bonkers, and I've no idea what to do about it."

So off I went, driving very slowly along the unlit road, looking for you in all the shadows at the side of the road. I got as far as the Ladybower Hotel, and thought you might have gone in there for some warmth, but you were nowhere to be seen. I carried on a bit further, but realised I was not going to find you, and turned back, thinking I'd ring A and E to see if you had turned up there again. But no, you weren't there this time. I'd tried your phone several times without any response, and later found out from a discussion with staff at 911 that it was still in your room.

After fretting all morning, I rang the police – again! – on Saturday afternoon, who took all your details. They rang back in the evening to say they had informed the Greater Manchester police, and the two forces would start a formal search early the following morning. A further call on Sunday morning was reassuring when I was informed that you had been spotted – by the landlord of the Ladybower Hotel as you had gone in for a drink the previous evening, and by two walkers who had passed you on the road. So, how far had you got, we wondered? The answer came at 1pm, when I took a reverse charge call.

"Mum?"

"Alex! Where are you, we've been worried sick?"

"I'm at Piccadilly station. Can you give the guy here your credit card details to buy me a ticket back to Sheffield?"

"Yes, hold on, I'll just get it."

I rang the police and apologised profusely for all the abortive work this had created, and they were quite gracious in dismissing this as an issue and confirming that I'd done absolutely the right thing in getting them involved. When I picked you up from Sheffield station, you had no explanation of why you had gone to Manchester, how you managed to get there, and where you had slept overnight. You gave me the silent treatment, and then continued to be difficult for the following week. I wondered what was so important about getting to Manchester – a bid for independence and freedom of movement perhaps? And had Manchester had more to offer than Goole?

A week later I found out that you had extended your horizons, when you rang one Tuesday night at 8 o'clock.

"Mum, can you come and pick me up?"

"Yes, where are you?"

"Lewisham."

"Lewisham? Alex what are you doing there? I can't drive down there and back now, it's three or four hours each way. When did you get there, and why?"

"I got the train down this morning, and have just been walking around all day and I'm really tired now."

"You need to get back to St. Pancras station to get a train back. Have you got a return ticket?"

"No. How do I get back there Mum?"

"The tube – you need to find a tube map at the nearest station. Can you find one?"

But I was really worried. You sounded very confused and I wasn't sure you were going to manage this. And there would not be many more trains back to Sheffield after 8 o'clock. So I got Dad on the case of looking at the tube journey from Lewisham to St. Pancras, while I found the train times to Sheffield. The last train was departing at 10.30pm. Dad rang you back with the tube details, but he wasn't convinced you were going to be able to do it, sounding very vague. So he suggested you get a taxi, and we would reimburse you whatever it cost when you got back, but you only had £15 cash on you.

"Ring Matthew, Gill – he can go and find him and get him back to St. Pancras in time." Matthew had arrived back in London, having finished his year in Taiwan, two days previously, and was staying with friends, Fiona and Owen, before returning to Sheffield. Matthew's phone wasn't responding, which was quite typical at that time. So I rang Owen's Mum in Sheffield, whom we knew, to get his number and tried that. He answered straight away, although there was a lot of noise in the background – it seems there was a bit of a party going on to welcome Matthew back. Matthew agreed to get a taxi to you and get you back to St Pancras in time – we just needed to get your exact location. So Dad rang you to get this, but could not get through. He kept trying for twenty minutes or so, before getting through eventually, to be told you were about to get the tube needed to get to St. Pancras. I rang Matthew to say all was well after all.

"It's 9.30 Alex, and the last train is 10.30, so don't dawdle. Ring us when you get there and we can pay for your ticket by phone."

"OK."

You made it, we bought the ticket, and there was time. We asked that you ring once on the train, so, after not hearing by 10.40, we rang you, and yes, you were on the train. I picked you up from the station at 1.15am, and gave you a big hug. But, once again, you had nothing to say about your motivation for going to London and remained silent.

"Alex, you can't keep wandering off to places for no apparent reason, and then get stuck. It's so worrying." You didn't respond to this, but I think I knew that you were probably thinking how much you needed to do things and go places on your own initiative, without having to rely on us. And who could blame you?

As usual, the next day I rang 911 staff to explain what you had done, and asked that they watch you carefully when I bring you back there. I also rang William, who arranged to visit you there the following day, at 3.30pm. At 3.15pm, however, 911 staff rang to say you had taken two day's tablets, had been unsteady, so they had called an ambulance. William agreed to speak with A and E staff, explaining your mental health condition and recent history, but had not heard back by 5pm, when he finished work. When I rang a little later the nurse refused to give me any information, saying I should ring your mobile. You answered straight away, and it seems you had been discharged, with no money, no coat and were walking home – seven miles from the Northern General. Dad set off to pick you up and bring you home.

Once more support staff at your flat sent you off to A and E on your own, without the means to get back safely; the Care Co-ordinator was off-duty before the situation was resolved; A and E staff thought, even after a conversation with William about your illness, they could send you home, and there's no reason why I should be told anything about it. And you were still angry, complaining about 'not being left alone'. While I pondered on how you would have fared these last few weeks, had you not had us on your case, like so many others we saw regularly in the various mental health wards, I worried where your drive for greater self-expression might take you next. Why was no-one else as concerned for your safety as we were? Did no-one feel the need to take some kind of pre-emptive action to prevent you from pursuing these perverse activities?

The next morning after I had taken you back to 911, I found your mobile at home, so took it round, to be told that you had left at 9 o'clock, without saying where you had been going. Without your phone there had been no contact with us or 911 by nightfall, and again it was freezing cold. 9 o'clock the next morning saw me calling the police again, and it only took them an hour and a half to locate you. You had been taken to Manchester Royal Infirmary very early this morning. A man on his way to work had found you slumped on the steps of the cathedral, with your ear cut by a broken bottle. Your second Good Samaritan, Alex. The great British public, at least, was on your side. I was impressed, on arriving at the Infirmary, that you had been seen by a mental health nurse, who came to speak with us when we picked you up. She said you had been in a very poor state, but had rallied very quickly, and your ear would soon heal. In the car on the way home I stifled any desire to ask, this time, what your motivation was for all this. Instead I burbled on about what a lovely sunny Sunday morning it was, and maybe we could go for a walk after getting you some lunch. You weren't in the mood for a walk, but opted to stay with us overnight.

First thing Monday morning I spoke to William about your exploits, and he arranged to come and see you that afternoon. I went to the pharmacy to pick up your medication and returned to find you in the kitchen with a knife in your hand. On seeing me, you turned to go down the hall, but too late, I had seen the blood on your neck. You were doing it again.
"Right, get your coat, I'll take you to hospital."
"No, Mum, I'm not going back there again. I'll be fine."
I could tell you were not to be persuaded, and Dad was away for the day, so I rang William for advice who told me to call an ambulance. Once again, you yielded to the formal appearance of the ambulance staff, and we all arrived at A and E at the Northern General shortly after two in the afternoon. The doctor explained you would need to go to a ward at the Hallamshire hospital across town to have your ear sutured, but that he thought a taxi transfer would be unsafe, given your state of mind, so we would need to wait for an ambulance slot.
A nurse dressed your ear temporarily while the doctor checked with the mental health ward on the procedure, reporting back that he'd told the Hallamshire staff that they needed to ring the Mental Health Duty Team when you arrived there so you could be assessed before discharge. He said we should be there within the hour, but two hours

later, we were still waiting. It was now 7.30pm, five hours since we arrived, and you were getting really cross.
"I've had enough of this, I'm off home."
"I'm sure it won't be long now, Alex, I'll just check."

I approached the nurse, rather gingerly, to ask how long it might be, as I couldn't keep you here any longer, so would ring for a taxi if it would be much longer. When she had dressed your ear hours earlier you had asked how long it would take for the ambulance, and she had responded very brusquely "Well it could be a while as we have lots of patients with worse conditions than a cut ear." There it was again – the lack of sympathy for the plight of a mentally ill person by A and E staff. Your bleeding ear wasn't the problem, it was why you had done it that was. And we needed to get the physical issue sorted before addressing the more worrying mental one. She would not let me get a taxi, but said she would ring to ask for greater priority, but despite her arguing with someone the other end, they would not give you priority. That was it. In the next half an hour you got up and walked out of the main entrance three times, with me and staff running after you. I was in tears by then and you were really angry. The third time you ran even faster, and the staff nurse had to call the security car to track you down. By the time they managed to bring you back, your ambulance had arrived, and we set off for the Hallamshire Hospital, arriving in the ward at 9 o'clock.

The doctor there immediately announced that your ear couldn't be treated immediately as another patient at the Children's Hospital was first in the queue for her attention. You were, understandably, incandescent at this, and I explained that we had already been waiting since 2 o'clock at the Northern General, and that you were likely to walk off if not treated now. So she rang the registrar to come in to fix your ear immediately. The nurse on reception then asked why you hadn't been assessed at the Northern General, where they have mental health staff. I explained the Doctor there had spoken with staff on this ward to tell them to ring the Duty Team to get someone out to the Hallamshire to do this when he arrived – but that was at 5 o'clock. They said they had no information on this, and did not have the Duty

Team's number, but I could use their phone to do this myself. I asked that they keep an eye on you to make sure you didn't just wander off and do something silly while I was on the phone. I didn't have the Duty Team number either, but I did have the number for Chester Ward, who were able to give me the number, and someone told me that a duty psychiatrist would contact me soon re an assessment. She rang ten minutes later, while the registrar was fixing your ear, and I urged her to be quick as I might not be able to keep you there much longer. I managed to contact Dad who would come and pick us up at 10.30pm. Dad and the psychiatrist emerged out of the lift together, and the four of us were ushered into a private room for you to be assessed.

I never understood how the professionals would be able to assess your mental state by just having a conversation, it didn't feel very scientific, but that is the only option available to them, it seems. In that initial discussion with our GP when Dad took you in to seek his help that first time, it had been touch and go as to whether he would be able to identify any signs of disturbance or abnormality underneath the veneer of reasonableness you were able to display then. Six years later, your illness had damaged that veneer somewhat, but still you had the ability to suddenly appear completely normal and reasonable, even after very distressing episodes.

"Hello Alex. I'm Doctor Abara, from the Duty Team. I want to find out how you are feeling just now, before we discharge you from hospital. Tell me, are you having any more thoughts of harming yourself?"

"No, I don't think so – I just want to go home. I'm tired."

"Yes, of course you are, and hopefully we can get you home soon. Why did you cut your ear again this morning Alex?"

"It just helps when I get feelings that I'm not a good person."

"But you're not going to do it again, you're sure?"

"No." I thought you would say anything she wanted to hear just to get out of there.

"Have you been taking your medication regularly?"

"Mostly."

"Mostly is not good enough, Alex, you really need to take them on a completely consistent basis if you want to avoid getting these negative feelings. Will you agree to do that?"

"Yes."

And so it continued for about fifteen minutes, but I think everyone was relieved when Doctor Abara announced that we could take you home – if you stayed with us, you could avoid being sectioned. We arrived back at the house at 11.30pm to find Matthew sitting on the front porch. He had arrived back from London, but had no key, having been in Taiwan for the last year. You were still angry, but very tired, and Dad agreed to delay going to bed until you had gone to sleep (which turned out to be 1.15am), while I sank into bed absolutely drained.

William, the Care Coordinator, rang the next morning to say the team psychiatrist, Doctor M, would visit you at 1.30pm. But, exhausted, you had been sleeping through most of the morning and so were still in bed. He tried to have a conversation with you, but you were not able to communicate properly. So he told me he would get the Home Treatment Team to work with you re keeping on the medication, and then try to get you to agree to having it by 'depot' (injected, slow-release) to ensure more stability in your condition. He was also going to try to get you prioritised on the waiting list for local Rehabilitation (intensive therapy and support), and seek short-term outpatient links with them first.

You didn't get up until the afternoon, and continued to be in an unsettled and agitated mood, although obviously still tired, and then you weren't prepared to go to bed at the normal time. At nearly midnight you insisted instead you wanted to go for a walk, and so Matthew agreed to go with you and managed to get you back home by 3.15am. The next day the Home Treatment Team rang to say they would visit, but I told them you were still asleep. When you woke up you agreed to take your medication, but continued to be angry, as you were the following day after the Home Treatment Team had left, following a discussion about your recent actions and mood. You insisted that I take you to Richard G's, and though this seemed a bad idea, there was no denying you, so I dropped you off, cautioning Richard G about your current mood, and saying that Dad would pick you up in a couple of hours. But when Dad arrived you refused to leave. I rang the Home Treatment Team but it was 6o'clock, after hours, and the duty staff member advised the only option for assistance was the police. And – once again – they managed to get you home. By this time we were all extremely anxious that it seemed we could not influence your behaviour or actions, and that we could not prevent any more undesirable, or even dangerous, activities you may have had in mind.

We awoke the next day, a Friday, to find you already up and really angry, and refusing to take your medication. The Home Treatment Team rang and I told them you needed to be in hospital as you were in a very unstable state. When they arrived it was a different team from the previous days, so neither of them had ever met you before. So I was rather short with them when, having had a conversation with you – and I could tell you were trying to display your more rational side – they declared they wanted to keep you out of hospital, that you did not appear to be at risk, and anyway, they thought there were no beds available. I had asked Matthew to join us so that he could add weight to my concerns, and describe how difficult your behaviour had been in recent days, and he explained all your recent difficult behaviour reinforcing my view that you needed to be in hospital for your own safety. Through all of this you remained silent, but I suspected you were taking some grim satisfaction from seeing the disagreement develop across the kitchen table, between Matthew and me and the two nurses. They then suggested that you could stay at a respite centre for the weekend, and you agreed to this, but when they rang the centre, they were told there was no space until tomorrow.

I had suggested that Dad was not involved, as I knew he might get angry. The three of us had agreed the previous evening that you needed to be somewhere safer than our house, and we were unsure about whether the professionals would respect our request as we had never actually asked that you be taken into hospital before. But he must have been listening to what was transpiring, and appeared in the kitchen to challenge them.
"Have you ever met Alex before?"
"No, this morning is the first time", one of them replied.

"So why do you think you know better than we do about whether or not he's at risk? How many more times do we need to get the police to help us?" And then he went on to list all your recent exploits, getting louder and louder, ending with "You're useless, aren't you? All of you are useless. You all say you're helping Alex to 'recover', and he just keeps getting more ill."

They, of course, looked extremely uncomfortable, and Matthew even more so. He felt the need to intervene.

"Dad, you can't talk to people like that. They are doing their best."

Then Dad rounded on him."Well, we can do without your input, Matthew. What do you know? You've only been around for a few days. We've been struggling for years, and getting nowhere. You just keep out of it."

I don't know what you were making of all this, Alex, as by this time I was almost in tears,

"We'll just go out to the car and make some enquiries, Mrs Holt" one of them said, "and let you know what we find."

Dad stormed off to the study, while I let them out of the front door and returned to Matthew, who was looking more than a little shell-shocked. Five minutes later they explained that there were no hospital beds available in Sheffield and the out-of-town beds available were only for those who had been sectioned. They would return to the office and take advice on what could be done.

Once they were gone, I could not hold it together anymore. You sloped off upstairs, having said nothing through all this, and Dad was 'barricaded' in his study. Matthew gave me a hug and I dissolved into tears.

"Oh Matthew, what are we going to do? Sorry about Dad – he's just beside himself. We both are. We can't go on like this."

I knew Matthew was hurting from Dad's reaction, and also from the way he'd been shocked by how bad your illness seemed now, since he left for his year in Taiwan. I knew Dad had run out of steam in his efforts to sort this out, and indeed, I would find that he remained in his study for much of the afternoon after this. And I felt, possibly for the first time, complete despair for our future. I also felt the need for an external intervention – someone outside we four who could take charge of the situation and help steer us through all this distress. But who could I ring? Various friends came to mind, both local and from further afield, whom I knew would be caring and sympathetic, but I had, for some reason, a strong feeling that this was a family affair, an issue that might be more appropriately tackled with the support of other family members. However my only close family member was my sister, and she was in New Zealand. She could do nothing from such a distance. I thought of Dad's sisters, with whom we had been quite close but our contact had diminished significantly over the years. Ainslie was in Luxemburg, again too far away, so I rang Kathleen, in Cambridgeshire.

"Hello, Kathleen, it's Gill"

"Gill – hello – how are you? Is everything all right?" She obviously suspected that it wasn't, since it had been a long time since I rang her, rather than Dad.

"No, Kathleen, our family is falling apart", I managed to articulate, amidst continuing sobs.

"Oh, Gill, what's happened?"

I gave her a summary of the awfulness of the last few days, and felt better just having shared this with someone beyond our tension-filled house. As you would expect she was very supportive, and suggested that I could come down to her at any time if I needed a break from it all. I explained that we needed to get you through this phase safely before I went anywhere, but that I may go down for a visit once that was achieved. She asked if Dad was around to speak to, but I knew he wouldn't want to talk to anyone, and then she asked after Matthew, who also then had a long conversation with her.

Afterwards, I sat quietly in the conservatory for a while as Matthew went upstairs to see how you were. He returned with the news that you were angry, but listening to music in your room. We were busy making some lunch, when you appeared in the kitchen saying you were going to Manchester, and headed towards the back door.

"Alex, don't be silly, you're not" I responded, pushing myself between you and the door.

"Why, am I a prisoner?" You spat out.

"Of course you're not, but you know what happened last time you went there." You're not well enough at the moment to be travelling out of town on your own."

"OK, well I'll go out this way then, and you darted towards the conservatory door."

Matthew and I exchanged troubled glances, as I rushed ahead of you, locked the door, and pocketed the key. We both felt unsure about whether we were going to be able to keep you safe. You gave me a hostile look and went back upstairs, which gave me the opportunity to lock the front and back doors also, to prevent any further attempts of yours to leave. What a situation – I had locked us all into our own house! This was the first time, in all our witnessing of your suffering over the years, that I was finding your behaviour potentially personally threatening.

Matthew had again followed you upstairs and spent some time with you, trying to calm you down, and returned to say that you seemed rather tired now and were quietly listening to music again.

"When are the Team going to ring back? There must be somewhere they can take him to keep him safe."

"Yes, I'm sure they'll ring soon, Mum. You're all on edge. Why don't you read a book or something to help you relax?" There was no way I was going to be able to concentrate on a book, so I went off to the lounge to watch a film on afternoon TV.

An hour or so later, I heard some knocking noises coming from the kitchen, so went to investigate. I found you amidst open cupboards, carefully emptying all the contents on to the worktops.

"What on earth are you doing, Alex?"

"Just thought it would be interesting to see what we've got. Thought I'd make some tea…"

I couldn't decide whether you were being deliberately provocative or genuinely undertaking a task that you thought was quite normal.

"Well, please stop, as I'll only have to put everything back again. I'll make some tea. You can help me if you want."

"No, it's fine. Just let me know when it's ready", and you disappeared upstairs again.

I could sense that there was still a black mood simmering under the surface, and that it was only a matter of time before it forced its way out, and worried that there was still no word from the Home Treatment Team. However, shortly after I started preparing tea, the call came.

"Hello, Mrs Holt, I'm pleased to say that a bed will be free at the Northern General by six o'clock this evening. Would you be able to take Alex in?"

"Yes, of course, but please could you talk to him to make sure he will go, as he's not been well disposed to me since this morning?"

"Yes, put him on."

I went upstairs and gave you the phone. You agreed with them that you would go.

"Right, I'll pack your bag, and we'll leave in about half an hour. OK?"

"Yes, OK", and you went downstairs, leaving me packing I gave Dad the news, and he looked tremendously relieved. Matthew agreed to come with us to the hospital. But when 5.30pm arrived, you refused to go.

"No, I'd prefer to go to Richard's for the evening. I fancy some different company for a change."

"Alex, you told the Team you would go to the hospital – they are expecting you."

"Yes, well I've changed my mind", and your voice was getting louder, By this time Dad and Matthew had appeared and the four of us were again all together, and tense, in the kitchen.

"And if you won't take me, I'll drive myself", as you snatched my car keys off the sideboard.

"No, you can't, Alex!" I shrieked, trying to snatch the keys back. You were glowering over me, and Dad pushed forward to intervene.

"Alex, stop this. I'm going to take you to hospital right now – give me the keys."

"No – I'm going to Richard's." You clutched the keys, defiant. And, by now, having put on all that weight from the medication, you were bigger than Dad.

"If you don't hand over the keys, Alex, we'll ring the police" Dad said.

"Go on then."

At this point, we hadn't noticed, but Matthew had slipped into the hall. But the stand-off continued. I watched in horror as Dad and you continued to challenge each other, with no progress made. Soon, however, we heard a knock at the front door, and Matthew appeared with two policemen in tow. I was so relieved he'd been there, wondering what would have happened had he not been, and able to act.

One officer guided you into the lounge while the other talked to Dad, Matthew and I, to assess what was going on. You and your officer soon reappeared in the hall, and he announced that the situation was clear. We all sat round while you insisted to him that you did not need to, so would not, go into hospital. I think I detected some grim enjoyment on your part from the attention you were getting, a bit of drama in your life.

"We have no authority, Alex, to force you to go, but we all think it would be the best course of action for you just now", he said.

"Well, I don't know why you're here at all" you responded, "you should be out chasing criminals."

"I agree with you, but our standing here trying to persuade you is preventing us from doing that, isn't it? And if you won't go with us now, I'm going to have to call an ambulance, as they do have the authority."

"OK, well do that then." You were at your most smugly defiant, and we all knew we could not persuade you otherwise.

So, twenty minutes later, two ambulance-men arrived at the door, and after a bit of banter with the police, one said to you,

"Oh I know you, don't I, I've picked you up before? Now you're going to come with us again, aren't you Alex?"

At this, you did look slightly taken aback, and agreed to go with them. We told you we'd come and visit the next day, and you said goodbye quite pleasantly – we had gone 360 degrees around the moods you could display these days, and you were now back at base.

I reflected how we could have avoided wasting a couple of hours of police and ambulance time if a member of the Team had been able to come and pick you up to take you to hospital – they too had the authority – but it was out of hours, so I assume no-one was available.

So, once again, we spent the last week of February 2013 visiting you every day in Lancaster Ward at the Northern General, taking you out for short walks around the block for some fresh air. It took several days for them to re-establish your medication and regime, before they announced that you were able to go back to your flat. But actually you chose to stay with us, and within days you managed to rediscover the difficult behaviour which had caused us such a problem only weeks earlier. One day, with now just Dad and me at home, as Matthew had gone to live with a friend in Glasgow for a while to see if he could establish some presence in the music scene there, we were again scared that we could not contain you at home. You were determined to get out and go who knows where to do who knows what.

One of us was 'on duty' at all times, but one Sunday you announced that your friend Richard J had suggested he come over with his girlfriend and that the three of you go out for a drink. This sounded great – normal socialisation with your best friend. But the timing had me worried after all your recent behaviour. However, I thought if you went to The Ranmoor – literally over the road from our house – it should work OK. They arrived from across town in a taxi, and it was really nice to see Richard J after not seeing him since I'd had to pick up your belongings from his house several years ago, after he'd thrown you out. I managed to have a quiet word with him while you went to get your coat, explaining how you were really going through a bad patch, with the key element being disappearing acts, so asked him not to let you out of his sight. However, only an hour later there was a knock at the door.

"Gill, I'm so sorry, but Alex has gone – we don't know where!"

"Oh dear – what happened?"

"Well, he'd run out of tobacco, so said he would just go to the off-licence next door, but didn't come back. Sorry, Gill, I know you said to keep a close eye on him and I shouldn't have let him go alone."

"It's OK, Richard J– you couldn't know just how difficult he's been – it's not your fault. Thank you for coming anyway." After he'd set off in another taxi, I was in the car, going down all possible routes away from the pub, having had no response from your phone. But it was never going to work – you could be anywhere. So – missing again, and unable to do anything but wait and see. It was a pleasant surprise when you arrived back about two hours later saying you'd been for a long walk around the park. However, we realised just how vulnerable we were to you just wandering off somewhere at any time.

"He needs to be back in hospital until his meds have stabilised" I said to Dad "we can't keep him safe here. I'll ring William."

"You're right, but forget William – that will take time to get any action. I'll take him myself back to Lancaster Ward . They'll have to take him back for a while till he's sorted." He managed to get you in the car and set off, but you two weren't on good terms.

I can only relay the outcome of this decision, as I was not there, but I can imagine how it panned out in my mind's eye, based on what Dad told me when he got back, about two hours later.

"Oh good, they've kept him in then?" I ventured to Dad, while noting the exasperated look on his face.

"Oh yes, but not without a fight – you wouldn't believe it – I've now been banned from entering the ward."

"Oh Andy, what did you do? You must have lost your cool?"

"Too right I did! I took him in and went into the office and explained how he'd been, so they had to keep him in a little longer, but they said they couldn't do that without a formal assessment of his state of mind. I told them that I could tell he was in a very difficult state of mind, so much that we didn't feel we could keep him safe."

"Good – and then what?" I ventured.

"Well of course I got angry at this point, and challenged the two staff there about how decisions were made in relation to budgets for care. I asked how much it cost to keep Alex in hospital per week, but they didn't know. So I suggested that they find out and then do a calculation about how many weeks he's been in hospital since he was turned down for

the locked rehab over two years ago, and compare the costs
– and that that wouldn't take account of all the A and E,
ambulance and police time necessary at various junctures,
sorting things out."
"And then what?" I asked again, as this seemed a
reasonable point to make.
"Well because I was shouting, and I might have thrown in a
swearword or two, they told me I had to leave the premises,
and they would not let me visit him for the foreseeable
future. They agreed to keep him in though."
Oh dear, I thought privately – I do wish Andy could keep his
temper in these situations. It really doesn't help to get angry
– better cool and persuasive, however difficult that may be.
But at least you were going to be safe. The next day I rang
to enquire after you and asked which ward you were in to
visit. They said they were keeping you in Lancaster Ward,
but that only I could visit – Dad was debarred. And, sure
enough, we received a formal letter the next day informing
us of this.

Meanwhile, you reacted to this situation with a whole month
of difficult and volatile behaviour, seemingly determined to
be non-compliant with all medication. You were in and out of
different hospital wards, being sectioned again, waving your
dinner knife at one of the hospital staff resulting in a transfer
to the secure unit in Bradford, and ending up back at the ITS
Unit in the Northern General – where the consultant there
who had first seen you about two years ago was charged
with assessing your condition. She was clearly shocked at
your deterioration, as she rang us at home to discuss it. Dad
answered, and had a fairly long conversation with her. She
explained that she was absolutely mortified by how much
worse your mental state was since she last saw you, nearly
two years ago, when she had recommended the rehab
option, and at how many times you had been re-admitted
consequently. The way the system works, she would not
have known the outcome of her recommendation, since the
decision was made by an unknown NHS panel, and was
communicated from them, to us, by the Community Health
Team. I think Dad felt vindicated by her response to the
situation being rather similar to his, and he was impressed
with her candour and understanding of our situation. She

empathised with his anger and said she'd advised that Dad's ban from visiting you should be revoked, which pleased him, of course. She considered that the only option left to have more impact would be to persuade you to agree to depot medication injections, and she would be recommending this to both you and your Community Health Team.

By this time, we were not the only ones involved in your care who were getting exasperated. With all these hospitalisations, the staff at 911 had hardly seen you, realised that you needed a more supportive environment than they were able to give, and knew that you had been on the waiting list for the ideal Beaufort Road facility for nearly two years, without seemingly receiving any priority. They hinted that the reason for this could be that first, you had at least a home with some support with them, and also that you always had a sound parental home as a backstop. But there was supposed to be a two-year limit to tenancies at their project, and so they proposed that they give you notice of the tenancy ending in a few weeks' time, at the end of April, to force the hands of the authorities. This seemed a rather desperate measure, but I could tell they had your interests at heart, and they said that if by the end of that period you had not been allocated a place at Beaufort Road, they would of course allow you to stay until you had. So they sent you a formal notice of this, copied to the Team.

With you safe in hospital again, we were able to reflect on the sheer awfulness of what you and we had been through in the last few months. We had been asking why you had not yet been successful on the waiting list for Sheffield-based rehab for which you had been on referral for nearly two years. With no clear answers, Dad threatened to write a letter of complaint about this, but was told that you were indeed on the list, and this would not help. Having spent much of my working life specialising in policy development in local councils, I had some clear-cut ideas about where the problems lay, and how these needed to be challenged to lead to improvement. So I decided that I could apply myself to producing a short summary of our recent experience, ending with some key questions in relation to service delivery in mental health, which could be used by the Care

Trust to review some areas of policy and practice. It took some time to produce this to my satisfaction, the most difficult aspect being reducing the events to a synopsis which was short enough to be read by a third party, but sufficiently clear to establish the basis for the policy questions. However, I managed to get the whole thing down to five sides of A4. The fifth page was this analysis:

So Who Cares ....?

(I started with a summarised diary of the awful events of February / March – the fateful trips to Manchester, the cuttings, the seven hours in A and E and the difficulties of getting the professionals to accept how bad things had become.) Then:

Why was all this possible? Is it that people don't care? Not so, in our experience:

The police – absolutely fantastic, showing great understanding and sensitivity.
The public – taking instant responsibility for helping an injured/vulnerable adult stranger.
A&E staff – struggling to find out how to deal with the mental not just the physical issue.
Ward staff – obviously concerned but puzzled about how to handle an unwilling patient.
Psychiatrist – committed to helping recovery, but limited capacity due to a 500 caseload.
Care co-ordinator – respected by Alex, and able to motivate him, but only intermittent contact.
Home treatment team – concerned, but no continuity of staff, & pressure of bed shortage.
Supported accommodation staff – kind and caring but unable to administer medication.

It's the system that needs improvement .... some questions:

- How can someone who has been sent from supported accommodation to A&E be discharged without letting anyone know, and with no phone to contact anyone or money to get home? And why can't their next of kin be informed of the situation when they ring to enquire?

- Why don't all medical doctors and nurses have at least a basic understanding of mental illness and the procedures for addressing it and getting appropriate support?

- Why isn't there always a mental health expert on duty at A&E? And if there isn't, why are you advised to take someone with a mental health issue to A&E?

- Why can a serious mental health condition not attract the same priority as a serious physical ailment for an ambulance transfer schedule?

- Why is there such a shortage of mental health beds in Sheffield?

- Surely it shouldn't be necessary to resort to police aid on four different occasions in a single month?

Prior to sending it to the Chief Executive of Sheffield Health and Social Care Trust, I sought some feedback from colleague trustees on our Sheffield Mind Board, some of whom were closely involved in the local mental health system – just to make sure that it seemed relevant, and had the appropriate tone. I was surprised to receive a response from the Trust in just four or five days, giving me some dates for meeting with him to discuss it. When I arrived I was surprised also by the fact that he had a colleague with him whom he introduced as the Head of Legal Affairs – it had not occurred to me that he was probably expecting me to threaten some kind of legal action against the Trust. However, they were both very charming as I took them through the main issues I had and asked them how they thought they would take my questions on board.

"Well, I think the best way to progress this is for you to make a formal complaint on any of the issues you outline here – to either our Trust, the Sheffield Hospital Trust responsible for A and E, or to both" said the CEO.

"Ah, but that's the point. I didn't want to make a complaint, as that would point the finger at the individual staff involved in some of these incidents, and I wouldn't want that. They're just operating a system that is sometimes flawed."

"Well that is how we could get to the bottom of some of these issues – that's what our complaints procedure is for."

"But I spent some considerable time condensing the experiences and analysing the lessons to be learned, for discussion – specifically as an aid to reviewing policy in these matters, not 'having a go at staff'. The really biggest issue, in our experience, is the lack of synchrony between your Care Trust and the Hospital Trust. Mental health issues do not confine themselves to office hours – indeed there is a far greater likelihood that something will develop outside those hours. Yet when it does, you can't help, and A and E is the only option, and they don't seem to be very well informed there on how to deal with these matters appropriately. In fact the police often seem more clued up and empathetic."

"Well, Mrs Holt, you'll be pleased to know that we actually have a bid in at present, to the Clinical Commissioning Group, to set up a Liaison Psychiatry Service, whose purpose will be to provide a round-the-clock mental health capability at the Northern General to support A and E. This is the result of a joint working party we have between the two organisations, tasked to make things seamless." This was interesting – we all consider A and E to be a 24-hour emergency service – but not, just now, for mental health issues in Sheffield, it would seem.

"Well that's good. Maybe I could send my report in to them and present it to one of their meetings?"

"No, I think you need to send details of the various occurrences as complaints to me and also to the CEO of the Hospital Trust, and we can take it from there."
At this stage I could tell there was no way around the complaints procedure, and this was so exasperating, when I had offered what I thought was a positive, rather than recriminatory approach to reviewing this catalogue of disaster. Undoubtedly they had received me with sympathy and respect, but there was no way I could summons the energy now to re-write our experiences in the form of complaints, even had I wanted to.

11. Window of Opportunity – May 2012 to December 2013

By this time it was mid-May, and the effect of the drug Clozapine on your condition was not obvious – you had been up and down since it started. There had continued to be some incidents, the need to involve the crisis team on one occasion after which you ended up back in Bradford and then back to Chester Ward when a bed became available. Here, they had decided to keep you in longer so that they could monitor in detail how you were responding to the Clozapine. They had allowed you leave on your birthday for another trip to Chester Zoo for the day, but the magic of the previous visit last year was not there – you were not so engaged this time. They planned a long transition back into the community, and, as usual, this involved spending increasing amounts of time, and then overnighters, with us at home, before a complete discharge back to your flat.

When I was preparing to set off for a week's tennis with friends in Portugal in early June, your disposition had hugely improved, and we had managed to have some good walks and outings during your hours back home. You'd had one of your first overnight stays with us and so joined Dad in seeing me off with a smile when the taxi came to pick me up for the airport. Devastation, then, to arrive back less than a week later to find you in critical condition in Intensive Care, covered in all that ice.

Dad had been really shocked at what happened, as your apparent improvement had continued apace in my absence. You and he had continued to spend some quality time, such that you had stayed with him for the weekend, arriving on Saturday morning and due back on Sunday evening. You had been in seemingly good spirits when you went to bed, and not late, so he was surprised when by 10.30am you had not appeared in the kitchen next morning and went to investigate. He found you in a semi-conscious state on the floor by the side of your bed, next to a pool of what must have been vomit, but which was bright turquoise. There were some bright turquoise tablets scattered on the floor.

When he returned from hospital in the evening, he picked up a voicemail from Chester Ward, wanting to know why you had not yet returned there. On returning the call, he was surprised at the response of the nurse to his shocking news. He had explained how surprised he was that you should try taking your life just at the stage where you seemed to have had a three or four-week period of significant improvement, and had actually started talking of going back to college again. Apparently, she said, this was quite common. When a sufferer had a prolonged period of improvement, they started to realise just how dreadful the effects of their illness had been, and how difficult it would be to get their life back on track. No-one had offered up this information to him beforehand or he would have been even more vigilant than usual in keeping an eye on you. Yet another learning point then – beware of significant improvement! As it was you were back in the ICU first thing on Monday morning to be told you were still in a very critical condition. You had inhaled some vomit and had developed pneumonia, and your temperature was dangerously high, so they had immersed you in ice-packs to try to accelerate the process. That was when he decided to ring me to come back from Portugal.

That Sunday, Alex, you were on the edge of life for the second time, and I recalled Dad's anguished announcement the last time, back in 2006, while we waited for the surgeon to stitch your wrists back together "Now he's done it once, it will be easier next time."And what a journey you and we had had in those seven years. However, Dad and I returned together to the ICU on the Monday morning, and were relieved to be told that you were now out of danger, but they would keep you in for a day or two for observation. You recovered physically quite quickly – you always did – the medical staff always said you had a strong constitution, able to withstand the onslaughts you made on your body. But, surprisingly, after such a serious incident, you also returned to a relatively positive disposition quickly.

Discharged from Intensive Care to Chester Ward again, however, nobody – Dad and I included – wanted to risk your returning down the road of non-compliance with medication and a resulting deterioration in your state of mind. And now there was a new course of action available – something only recently introduced under the mental health acts into the options for trying to enforce compliance – a Community Treatment Order. The sectioning process you had been through hitherto kept you in hospital for treatment until they felt you well enough to be discharged. The new measure allowed you to be discharged to live out in the community, subject to conditions they thought appropriate. In your case, these would be that you agreed to have regular depot injections of your medication, thereby maintaining a level of stability in your mental state, and that you continued to respond positively to the Team's care programme. We knew how resistant you had been to the idea of enforced medication, but really we had run out of options – and you were running out of hope. Reluctantly you agreed, and remained a fortnight in hospital for the duration of the first depot.

But also there was another positive element to this state of affairs – the Community Treatment Order could not be fully implemented unless you had a home back in the community to go to – and your tenancy at 911 had now expired – the period of notice they had given you had expired while you were in hospital. So it was agreed that your position on the waiting list for Beaufort Road needed to be reviewed urgently. Meanwhile, there would be a transitional period in which you would be gradually discharged to our care for increasing periods of time.

By now it was the end of July and we were having very lucid conversations about how to go about sorting out your future. This was obviously very encouraging, but I did retain an underlying concern, remembering what the nurse at Chester Ward had told Dad – how you might be finding the gulf between the life you had hoped for and the one that you were in at the moment unbridgeable. So, once again, we agreed that you should have another go at some studying, but this time, you said, you wanted something that would prepare you in some way for work. You were back in the mindset of 'all I need is a job and then I'll be fine', but I knew that that was too easy. However – certainly a good idea to work on. So we got a prospectus from Sheffield College and reviewed the possibilities open to you, and set up a meeting with a course leader in the Business Department. He was incredibly sympathetic to your position, and talked things through with you, explaining that because of your illness, you would have access to various support options in the college if you ever needed them. We followed his advice and agreed to register you for an Accounting Trainee course when the time came in the summer, for a September start. This was a course run mostly on a day release basis for people in work, being supported by their employers to achieve a professional qualification, and was very well respected and valued in the commercial world. I knew this because in my work I had organised for several finance staff to follow this route over the years. You were really impressed when he added that as soon as you gained the first-year part-qualification (provided you passed your exams of course), you would be eligible – and marketable as such – to undertake accounting tasks for companies on a freelance basis should you wish.

"But I'm not sure I could operate well in an office environment just now" you said, echoing what I was thinking. "No, I realise that might take a little time" he responded, "but that's the beauty of this kind of work. You can work from home and the only contact you need have, if you wish, is with the commissioner of the work." He was very understanding, and I wondered if he had been through this process with others like you, Alex. Anyway, we both left the college quite buoyed up and we discussed how we needed to get you involved in other more purposeful activities. You had been promised support to this end from the 'SORT' (Sheffield Outreach Team) – people attached to your CMHT who would seek to engage you in suitable hobbies and sociable activity, but this had not yet materialised as you had been in and out of hospital so much. But we agreed we would ask William to set that up for you. Also I was aware of a range of activities provided by Sheffield Mind, and would explore these with the staff there the next day. Things were looking up. Again I had the feeling that there was the prospect of working towards your recovery, and this time I felt that you were having more positive thoughts also.

It was important to keep up the momentum, so the next day I rang William and he set up a session with you to discuss what was on offer through the SORT team. Unfortunately, though, he also told me that he had recently acquired another job and would be leaving in a few weeks, so you would be allocated a new Care Co-ordinator. This felt a bit of a blow, as you had developed and retained a positive relationship with him, through all the troubles of the last couple of years, and I thought it might be difficult for a new person to assimilate your complex back-story and get to know you sufficiently well. However, it couldn't be avoided.

I made an appointment with one of the managers at Sheffield Mind, and discussed the kind of activities you might be interested in/suitable for. I was hoping that they would enlist you as a volunteer worker in the office, since this was a service they provided for mental illness sufferers who were approaching recovery, to help them get work experience, but he thought that it was too early for you, and that you would find this too challenging. In the end you completed an application giving details of your illness and interests, and registered for two activities – the Social Cafes and the 'Food for You' project. The former was a series of three community bases across the city where cafe sessions were held for a couple of hours on a weekly basis, where participants could meet socially and potentially strike up friendships, and where there were volunteer workers, mostly grateful former recovered clients, who would be available to talk to also. The latter was a home cooking class held in a community centre on Tuesday mornings, where a volunteer (again a former client) helped clients discover/rediscover how to cook healthy and nutritious meals. You were particularly interested in this one, since you were acutely aware of how your culinary standards had slipped into a significant reliance on take-aways and junk food. You engaged with both these activities, but less regularly and enthusiastically with the cafes, as I think you were more taken with practical activity for a purpose than a purely social event.

This really did have the feel of a new beginning. Dad felt it too. We discussed how much more relaxed you were, and how you were more often initiating conversations with us rather than just responding. We didn't notice this immediately, but you were also a little bit subdued a lot of the time. Dad was so pleased with your current presenting state that he agreed – for only the second time in six years, since our aborted trip to Morocco, to spend a few days in Pembrokeshire to celebrate my sixtieth birthday. We would be away for only four days, three nights, and you had indicated you would be OK. The team knew about these arrangements, and were primed to take a call if anything went badly.

We spent the first two days with Sue and Alan, our friends from Liverpool, in a lovely hotel overlooking Saundersfoot beach, and enjoying a joint birthday meal. Sue is my 'twin', we were born on the same day, and we always tried to get together around our birthdays. On the second morning (my birthday), sitting on the roof terrace outside our room on a beautiful sunny morning, I rang you.

"Hi Alex. How are you?"

"I'm fine, Mum – happy birthday!"

"Thank you. It's lovely here, so we are going for a walk along the coast shortly before having a special dinner tonight. Do you have any plans?"

"Not really. I'll just watch TV tonight, but maybe try to catch up with Richard G tomorrow."

"Ok. We should be back early afternoon on Wednesday, so would you like to come over for tea?"

"Yes, probably. See you then."

This was a routine phone conversation by most standards, but was quite a rarity from our perspective. It was not very often I could put the phone down and feel fairly relaxed that you would not come to any harm in our absence. And so we were able to enjoy also the next two days, spent with Hilary and Tim at their holiday home in St Florence – a village outside Tenby. For the first time in over six years, Dad and I enjoyed a swim together at Swanage beach on a beautiful summer day.

Shortly after our return, you were assigned a new Care Co-ordinator, Chris, who seemed pleasant, if a little young, and I worried whether he would be experienced enough for the seriousness of your condition and difficult behavioural patterns. He explained that there was a waiting list to access SORT (the outreach activity team), and it might be a while before you could start with them, but that he could involve you in a drop-in centre, and he started to take you there on a weekly basis, after your regular appointment with him. Every other session, still, on a fortnightly basis, he would administer the medication injection and, despite your continuing better humour, and me telling you how much better you were with it than before, you made it quite clear that you still resented this strongly.

Meanwhile, the Care Trust had gone into action in response to your suicide attempt. They were obliged to review what had happened since at the time you were still on a Section, and so still their responsibility, even though it happened in our house. They invited Dad and me to meet with the authors of the review – two medical staff who had no connection with your care. They asked what we thought could have been done to avoid your overdose. In relation to the actual process of your gradual discharge from hospital – which is what they thought was our main concern – the only response we could offer was that the staff, on releasing you to Dad's care at home, could have cautioned him more appropriately about your potential vulnerability at that time. When Dad informed them afterwards of your overdose they had not seemed very surprised.
"Oh dear, well that is often the case, of course" the nurse had told him "when patients get back on to regular medication and can view their situation more rationally, they can become distressed by how ill they have been, and the challenge of trying to get their life back on track."
We suggested that it would have been more helpful to warn Dad of this possibility in advance so that he could have been even more vigilant with you than usual. However, we expressed our main concerns as more fundamental issues underlying your long-term recovery – the lack of progress in relation to both accessing support from SORT (the Social Outreach Team), and also a tenancy at Beaufort Road, both of which you had been promised but had failed to materialise. You had been on the waiting list for the latter for two years. By now this was August and the staff intimated

they would forward a copy to us for comment, but said it might take a while as some critical staff were on holiday.

Then there was some good news! We heard that a tenancy had become available at Beaufort Road and we could view it in a few days' time. We had always thought the location was ideal – close to the Broomhill shopping centre and only a three-stop bus ride into town one way and to our house the other. The flat itself was fine – a good-sized bedsitting room with a small kitchen off one end, and a separate bathroom. You would have your own key worker there who would, in consort with Chris, arrange and support your participation in social activities, and socialisation within the complex was encouraged by regular on-site events and activities. Dad and I were really pleased, but somewhat disconcerted that you did not seem to be so impressed. In retrospect, I realise you were finding it increasingly difficult to be motivated by any developments, having been so often disappointed in the past. Nevertheless, Dad and I discussed that we at least felt more positive now that you would be in a more appropriate and supportive environment. Since your hospitalisation there had been no contact with your new 'friends' around 911 and this seemed likely to continue.

One emerging issue, though, did continue to trouble us. As you had improved with regular medication through the summer, we had had more rational conversations with you about your future. For the first time you had started to question how your personal situation might unfold.
"Mum, I'm never going to have my own place am I?" you asked, as we were sitting having a coffee in the conservatory.
"What – you mean buy your own house?"
"Yes, or even rent a little flat that I can call my own."
"Well of course you will, but just not yet. But once you feel settled in Beaufort Road you can start to get used to being independent and looking after yourself. And if your course goes well, at the end of the academic year you should be able to get some contract work. Then you will be ready to either rent somewhere – or buy if you prefer – Dad and I would help you buy somewhere. You did not look too convinced by my response so a few days later I opened the

conversation again, focusing on the property pages of the Sheffield Telegraph, to make the possibility seem more real. We perused what was currently available and you decided you would prefer a small house close to us rather than one of the hundreds of flats available around the city centre. Meanwhile, you moved into your new supported flat, and we felt this was the beginning of a more stable period all round: you were in appropriate accommodation with support, you were going to start a course towards securing a qualification that would open up work possibilities, and you were guaranteed continuous benefit from medication towards managing your condition.

You seemed to settle into your flat and I was so optimistic about your improved disposition that I thought you might feel able to join us for a belated sixtieth birthday celebration I had organised – lunch at the local wine bar with Dad's family, followed by an evening party at home. Matthew had come up from London with a friend of his to join us. You had said you were not up to it but the night before I rang you.

"Hi Alex. I just thought I'd check whether you would come over tomorrow. I know you won't like the party with all our friends, but it would be so nice to see your cousins again, so you could just come for lunch? Dad would pick you up and drop you back afterwards."

"Mum, I really can't, you know I don't like being among a lot of people."

"I know, but these are your relatives, people you know, and they would love to see you again. We've got a private room booked, so you won't need to see anyone else. It would mean a lot to me, Alex."

"Sorry Mum but really I just can't do it. I'll come round the day after instead?"

"OK, love. I'll see you Sunday. I'll make us a nice roast."

"Yes, have a nice time, Mum, and I'll come over Sunday." Of course I enjoyed my celebration anyway, but I couldn't help comparing this with my fiftieth birthday – when I had also had a party, to which you and your friends had come, and we had danced together. I didn't know then that a few weeks after that occasion, back in 2003, the unravelling of your life would start with our finding out that you had failed the critical exam at university and were no longer a student.

With the beginning of September a new routine began that was very reassuring. On Tuesday mornings I would pick you up from your flat and take you to your food preparation sessions in Nether Edge. We would arrange to meet up for a coffee and/or a walk on either Wednesday or Thursday, and on Friday you attended your accountancy course all day, and I would enjoy having a meal ready for you in the evening. I remember getting very wistful on those Friday afternoons, as it felt like a bit of a time warp – it reminded me of the autumn of 2001 when you worked at John Lewis seven days a week, saving money for your gap year trip to Australia, and I would muse then on how grown up you seemed to be, coming home from 'proper work' every night! At that time, of course, I was at work, so the only days I could have a meal ready for you were Saturdays and Sundays. But I really enjoyed that experience, and wondered what my younger self (and indeed yours) would have thought then of the situation we were in now. An enduring factor, however, was the importance of Liverpool football club in your life, and so there would be many Sundays and mid-week evenings when we would all watch the match together. Football generally was a constant topic of conversation between you and Dad.

The only obvious 'fly in the ointment' was your fortnightly visit from Chris, who would deliver your enforced depot medication, which still infuriated you. I could understand how this lack of control would affect you, but I knew from experience that this was perhaps our only hope for keeping you stable. However, there was another development causing concern to Dad and me. We were both enjoying spending more 'normal' times with you – by that I mean stress-free occasions out walking or just sitting at home, and chatting with you about everyday topics. But we conferred that we had both been involved, on more than one occasion, in conversations with a worrying aspect. They would go something like this.
"Mum, what will happen to me when you and Dad aren't here anymore?"
"What – you mean when we're dead?"
"Yes."

"Well, hopefully that will be quite a time off yet, and there is plenty of time for you to get yourself sorted. You're on your way with the accountancy qualification, which can lead to a job, and you have a good flat with support to help you get back on your feet. Once you feel a bit more solid living on your own, Dad and I have said we'll help you get your own place."

"But what if it doesn't work? What if I fail my exams?"

"Anyone in any situation could worry about that Alex, you just have to work on it as best you can. You've said the first two or three weeks have gone well, so that's a good sign."

"But I've lost all my friends. I've only really got Richard G, and I've managed to upset him so much he's really cagey with me sometimes."

"You can make new friends at your flat – there are social activities to help with that. And what about your course?"

"They are all day-release people who already work and I can't really talk to them."

Dad and I realised how dependent upon us you had been – for social interaction as much as a roof over your head. We had started the process towards your greater independence through the college course and through the Sheffield Mind food workshops, but we really needed to push harder on the socialisation issue. Having waited so long to be allocated a place at Beaufort Road, and with the prospect of living in an appropriate and supportive environment, it seemed that you had given up on trying to develop a more self-contained life for yourself. I continued to buy the Sheffield Telegraph occasionally so that we could look together at the properties available for sale, to maintain the notion that you would be able to have your own place in good time. But it was clear to me that you were far from convinced.

At this time, Dad drew my attention to a new habit he had noticed you developing.

"Have you noticed, Gill, how Alex has taken to watching the 'Friends' repeats on TV just about every day?"

"Yes, I suppose I have. I keep hearing the theme tune while he's sitting in the lounge."

"Well, it can't be just a coincidence, can it? I'm sure he's remembering how he used to be – having regular contact and banter with his friendship group – something he hasn't had for years now."

This was very observant – I hadn't noticed, or at least reflected on its significance. With your new equilibrium, no doubt you were considering whether, and how, you could enjoy such a sociable existence again. But what could we do to help you answer that question?

The fortnightly depot injection was delivering its promise of keeping your personality stable – there was no strange behaviour, no worrying outbursts, nor disappearances, and this was massively reassuring and a welcome break, for Dad and I, from the tensions and worries that had filled many of our days for some years now. But you still had little informal social interaction, and several phone conversations between Chris and me had not yet resulted in your being engaged with the Outreach team. One day Chris dropped you off at our house, as you were coming for tea.

"What a waste of time that was!" you scoffed.

"Where have you been?" I replied.

Chris is telling me that I need to socialise more, so he took me to a community centre in Hillsborough to a pool group that meets there each week."

"OK, so what's wrong with that?"

"I don't want to hang out playing pool with people I've got nothing in common with. I need to do something more constructive, more interesting."

"Did he not mention getting the Outreach team involved – they've been promising that for ages, but nothing materialises. Last time I spoke to him he said it wouldn't be long before they could take you on?"

"No. But I'm seeing Dr M next week, so he may know something."

"Right, can I come with you then, and we'll see what's going on?"

"Yeah, fine."

When the day came it was unfortunate that you seemed a bit withdrawn, not very talkative, and Dr M commented on this when he was unable to get much response to his questions about how you were feeling. I think you were probably always a little sullen in your dealings with the professionals as you never lost your resentment at having enforced medication. However, I was determined to get some movement in relation to the Outreach team.

"Dr M, I've had several phone calls with Chris, asking why Alex is not yet involved with the Outreach team. He keeps saying that they'll be able to get involved soon but can't ever give a specific date."

"Yes, Mrs Holt, we will be getting them involved, but I think it may be better not to over-face Alex with too many commitments too quickly – he needs some time to settle into his college course."

"No, I think you're mistaken. He's had six or seven weeks at college now, and doing fine with it – aren't you, Alex?"

A rather unenthusiastic "Mmm" from you.

"And he goes to a cooking group at Sheffield Mind every week, too, and really enjoys it, don't you Alex?"

This time we just had a nod from you – you were not going to engage fully, unfortunately. But I continued.

"He needs something more stimulating than going to the drop-in pool group Chris took him to last week. And you will recall at the Tribunal meeting in August, I emphasised then how important it would be for Alex to have proactive support from the Outreach team, and my husband made a plea that Alex would not be 'allowed to languish alone in Beaufort Road'. The Chair was moved to specifically refer to the importance of this in his decision statement, describing the following weeks as a 'window of opportunity' to motivate Alex into engaging with more positive activities. And now it's mid-November, and Alex is only engaged in things that he and I have set up."

"OK, Mrs Holt. Chris and I have discussed this and we have a particular Outreach worker in mind who we think will be very appropriate to work with Alex, so I'll speak to him to see if he can fix a date for a first appointment with her."

"Thank you, that sounds good, so shall we wait to hear from Chris?"

"Yes, he'll be in touch."

Sure enough, at your next session with Chris he had acted on this and explained to you that the team was very busy so he had fixed a first appointment with the worker they had in mind, but it would be mid-December. At least we now had a date – and before Christmas, so hopefully you could really get going in 2014.

Christmas was approaching and we all had a quiet few weeks, enjoying this new trouble-free routine: of weekend football and roast dinners; midweek cookery group, coffees, walks and lunches; and the Friday college day when I would have dinner ready for you. As I said, I loved doing that, it felt so normal – and you talked quite positively of your days there. On one occasion you explained that you would be having your first exam the following week, at the end of term, to check that you and the other students were making satisfactory progress.

"How are you feeling about that Alex? Do you feel reasonably confident?"

"Yes I think so. I'm slightly worried that it's organised online and I've not done that before, and I'm not very fast or good at typing. But they explained the best way of revising this next week to prepare so I know what I need to do."

The following Friday you explained over supper that you felt the exam had gone well, and that you would get the results next week. Sure enough, as you took your coat off the following week, you handed me a sheet of paper – your results. I was stunned. In the first column were ten different elements of the test. Against all but one there was a tick in the box entitled 'Exceeded the standard required', and in the other a tick against 'Met the standard required'.

"Alex that's fantastic – well done. We need to celebrate this", as I went out to the garage to fetch a couple of beers. I came back with two bottles to find you looking at me rather bemused.

"Aren't you pleased Alex? This is a great first step towards you getting a job!"

"I suppose so" you responded, demonstrating little enthusiasm.

"I don't understand why you're so blasé about this."

"Well, nothing seems to matter anymore." In a few days' time, this phrase would start to reverberate around my head on a regular basis.

In the relative peace and normality of the last couple of months this 'flatness' had become a worrying background facet of your personality. You were placid, seemed reasonably content, and engaged in everyday conversations with Dad and me, but you were never animated about anything – either positive or negative. Even when Liverpool FC had managed to turn around a losing match to win in the final minute, you looked pleased but did not get excited as you would have in the past. Dad and I discussed this and hoped that the outreach worker you would see shortly to start a programme of planned activity in the New Year would be able to capture your imagination and generate greater interest. Knowing this dulling effect was a side effect of your depot medication, you had set in motion an appeal against the Community Treatment Order, which had taken place on 9th December. You were not pleased with the outcome, nor with Dad and I agreeing with the professionals you should stay on it a little longer. However, Dad and I had stressed how important we thought the non-medical side of your treatment was, and the Team members agreed that you would have an activity programme developed with the SORT Team. The chair of the tribunal reinforced this message, emphasising in his outcome announcement that the chair of the previous tribunal in August had identified this time, on ensured continuous medication, as a 'window of opportunity' for you to be motivated by appropriate social and purposeful activities.

I had tried to enlist your help in putting up the Christmas decorations and tree, but to no avail. You asked what I might like for Christmas and I suggested a recently published biography of Andy Murray, following his long-awaited success at Wimbledon that summer. At this stage you were staying at our house more often than going back to your flat. I don't think you could find the energy to try to settle into yet another flat, get to know another set of flatmates, and this, along with continued conversations with Dad and me about what would happen to you when we were gone, was another source of worry.

12. Missed Opportunity – 11th December to 2nd

January 2014

Quite late on a Wednesday night, I was dealing with some emails on my computer when you came over and gave me a big hug.

"Goodnight Mum – I think I'll turn in early" – and a really big smile.

"Night night Alex." I was really surprised, as such shows of affection were still quite rare. "Give your dad a hug, too, on your way up – he'll appreciate it."

The next morning I went to my art group before you were up, leaving Dad clearing up leaves in the garden. I returned earlier than usual, shortly before twelve, to find Dad's car gone and no-one around. I went upstairs to check you weren't still in bed, and you were. You were lying in bed, staring at the ceiling and trembling all over.

"Alex, what's the matter?!" I shouted as I pulled back the duvet. You couldn't speak but I noticed a half empty pack of turquoise tablets on the floor by the bed.

"Oh no, Alex, not again. What have you done?" as I took hold of your shoulders and tried to pull you up.

You looked spaced-out but also startled at seeing me. You were trembling and cold, so cold. I managed to pull you to a sitting position on the bed, but could see that your feet were blue. I ran to the chest of drawers and grabbed some thick ski socks which I pulled onto your feet. "Can you walk Alex?" I queried, as I tried to pull you upright.

"I....I'm not sure..." you murmured, still looking spaced out. You did manage to stumble around with my arm around you and we managed to get you downstairs. I sat you down at the kitchen table and poured some warm water from the kettle into a mug not knowing whether this would help – but I had to get you warm. You were still sipping this, and I was rubbing your feet to try to get the circulation back when Dad walked in.

"Alex, you look dreadful, what's happened?"

I explained, and pointed to the turquoise tablets on the sideboard.

"Alex, how could you do this.....again.......after last time....?"

"I'm sorry, Dad, I just thought they'd help me sleep better....."

"But you know you have Diazepam to take for that – and you have no clue what that stuff off the internet can do" he rejoined.

And so started another of those motivational conversations, where Dad and I would try our best to convince you that you were heading back to a normal life – and how you were going to get there. All the while I was rubbing your cold hands, with your feet soaking in a bowl of warm water. Again – amazingly – your body seemed to emerge out of whatever state the tablets had thrust it into. I made you some tea and toast, which seemed to go down well. You were still quite shaken, though, and I needed some advice on what to do, so rang Chris. Unusually, he was in the office, and said I should take you to A and E so that they could undertake the usual tests to establish if there was any permanent damage. Once again they needed to keep you in for observation, even though everything seemed to be stable. When I left at teatime you expressed concern about the prospect of another weekend in the Northern General.

"Mum, don't let them keep me here after tomorrow – you know they don't discharge anyone over the weekend and I can't bear to be in here any longer."

"OK – I'll speak to Chris first thing tomorrow and see what's going to happen", and gave you a kiss.

Once again Chris was there when I called and said that he had arranged for you to be interviewed later that day to assess your state of mind – and to consider whether you could be discharged. He rang back later to say that you had a clean bill of health physically, and that the mental health assessors considered you were in a more sound mind, not seemingly 'responding to external stimuli' (hearing voices), but noted that your energy level was low, and that you had presented as 'flat'.

"He's really desperate to avoid being left in hospital for the weekend. If they discharge him this afternoon, he can stay with us all weekend. We have nothing planned so can keep a constant eye on him" I explained. After several conversations between them, Chris, and me, they agreed that you could be discharged into our care for the weekend, and that Chris would come for a review session with you on Monday,

It was a strange weekend. To avoid just 'hanging around' we went out for lunch on the Saturday to the Norfolk Arms. You didn't feel up to walking so we drove there and had a pleasant meal. Of course under the surface Dad and I were completely stressed out, but anxious not to 'rock the boat' with you. So it was as if nothing had happened. We didn't know what to do. What to say. How to react. We all had a quiet evening watching TV. At one stage you asked what I had done with the remaining tablets – which horrified me. "How can you ask Alex? Of course I have thrown them away! What do you expect – you know they are a disaster! Why are you continuing like this, Alex? You're doing well in your course. You're not hearing voices anymore. You've got an appointment with the outreach worker next week. And Matthew will be home soon so we can have a nice family Christmas."
"Yeah...but nothing seems to matter anymore..." That phrase again.
"Oh Alex" I said, hugging you. You hugged me back but said nothing.
"C'mon, things really are looking up." Still you said nothing. After you'd gone to bed I stayed up later than usual and checked up on you first. Dad stayed up even later and checked on you too. I was up at 7am and pleased to find you still sound asleep.

We had your favourite for lunch – slow roast lamb shoulder – followed by rice pudding, after which we watched the Liverpool v Spurs match on Sky Sports. It was a great game. Liverpool were 4-0 up when I dozed off – the lunch and wine taking their toll.
"Mum, Mum, it's 5" you shouted.
I was instantly awake in time to see the replay. And also to note that you were animated – if only slightly. After the post-match analysis Dad entertained us with his favourite impersonations – of Steven Gerrard's heavily scouse

response to the win, and Gary Neville's Mancunian tones on how Liverpool won the game. You agreed to go Christmas shopping with me the following morning, and after our late checks once again you slept through till about 8.30am.

The next morning in town you were dragging your heels a bit after I had bought a few things in John Lewis, and was heading for Marks and Spencer. You suggested that you go to HMV and meet me back in the M&S cafe a little later. I was rather anxious about letting you out of my sight, but you seemed in fairly positive spirits, so agreed. After half an hour I answered my phone.

"Mum... where are you?"

"I'm still in M&S. What's the matter – where are you?"

"I'm outside the cafe, can you come?" I heard your agitation coming through.

"Yes of course – I'll be up there in two minutes."

I found you pressed against the wall in a corner outside the cafe, trying to be invisible. Once we sat down with our drinks you seemed to settle down.

"Are you OK?"

"Yes, Mum. I just haven't been in big busy shops for a while, that's all."

When we arrived home you went straight into the lounge to wrap the presents you had bought. Dad sought you out and announced you needed some new clothes for Christmas.

"You need some better jeans than those, Alex, and that sweatshirt has definitely seen better days! Let's go down Ecclesall Road and have a look."

"Chris is coming round at 2pm" you replied.

"Yes – we'll be back by then though."

You returned at 1.30pm with some large paper carriers, and Dad looking pleased with himself.

When Chris arrived, you elected to have your review session with just the two of you, rather than involving Dad or me. Nearly two hours later you emerged from the lounge and I let Chris out. He said it had been a positive discussion, that you seemed in better spirits, and you had agreed with his suggestion that you should start spending more time back at your flat, so taking advantage of the socialisation opportunities there.

"What's for tea Mum?" you asked, cheerily.

"I'm just getting it on. I'm afraid it's only the rest of the lamb from yesterday, though. How did it go with Chris?"

"Fine. He says I need to be less reliant on you and dad. I should be spending more time at Beaufort Road. He's right, and there's an open supper there tomorrow, so I'll head back there this evening."

"OK – if you're sure....?"

After tea you asked Dad if he'd give you a lift back to the flat.

"Well, it's only two stops on the bus Alex, and I'm going up to Grange shortly. I need to make sure the garden's sorted properly before Christmas."

"OK, I'll take you Alex."

"No, it's OK Mum, Dad's right. I'll get the bus, but have you any change?"

I gave you a few coins, saying "And don't forget – talk to Hanif (your key worker at Beaufort Road) when you get back. He's there to help you get back into things."

"Yes, will do, Mum."

"And shall I pick you up tomorrow to take you to the food group? I'm going to a meeting at Sheffield Mind anyway for 10am."

"I'll probably take the bus, but I'll text you if I change my mind."

"OK – maybe see you tomorrow then."

A quick kiss for Dad and me and you were gone.

"What do you think, then?" Dad asked me, "Is he going to try harder to settle into Beaufort Road?"

"I think he will. I'm sure Chris will have spoken to Hanif to get his active help in this – and he also has an appointment on Thursday to start a programme, at last, with the Outreach team."

"Let's hope so. Things have got to start getting better soon. Anyway, I'm off to Grange now. It's going to be fine weather tomorrow, so I should get it all done and be back tomorrow evening."

"OK. Take care on the motorway." A kiss and Dad too was gone.

So – I was on my own. It's hard now to describe how I felt. Anxiety – yes, as always, more worry about whether you really would engage with things at Beaufort Road now. A bit of hope, perhaps – was Chris right about your apparent positive spirit? Yes, you'd been quite lively and chatty since he'd left. But then you had not given us any prior indication that you would do what you did last Thursday. But also – a bit – relief. The stress of the last few days had been palatable. You'd taken action again that could have taken you from us. Dad and I had been on edge all weekend, trying to be sure we kept you safe. We had. But would you do something again? I was sorely tempted, as so often in the past I would have, to ring or text you to check you were OK. But, no, I thought – you'd only been gone an hour or so and would be irritated by my fussing over you when no doubt Hanif or a colleague back at Beaufort Road would, at this very moment, be having a conversation with you, following Chris's session with you earlier.

I considered how to spend the evening and decided that a bit of escapism was in order. There was nothing much on TV, but sitting next to the TV I spotted a video of Andy Murray winning Wimbledon. I had watched it immediately on purchase, back in August, but decided that a re-run would be decidedly relaxing and therapeutic. And it was. I got lost in the euphoria of that Sunday afternoon back in August. After following Murray's progress closely since he started out as a teenager, it had been so gratifying to see him win, at last, the ultimate tournament. It really did help to take my mind off the recent stressful events. Then I retired for an early night, as I and the Deputy Chair were interviewing for a new CEO for Sheffield Mind tomorrow morning. Again I considered giving you a call, but thought better of it.

I awoke the following morning with a distinctly uneasy feeling. I told myself it was because it was the first morning you had not been with us since your actions of the previous Thursday, so all I needed to do was ring and see if you wanted a lift to the Food Group. I'd feel better by seeing you. I tried first at around 7.45am, but knew from experience that if you were fully asleep the ring would not wake you, but then twice more – at 8am and 8.15am – but to no avail. So then I rang the office at Beaufort Road.
"Hello. It's Gill Holt here. I've been trying to get hold of Alex for a while now. We have an appointment at 9.30am, but

he's not responding. I wonder if you could see if you can get a response?"

"OK – I'll go round now and ring you back."

"I'm afraid he's not answering his door – maybe you could try again later?"

"No, I really need to be sure he's OK. I'll come over now."

Fifteen minutes later I was in the office with the woman on duty, having tried ringing the bell at your flat.

"I've just tried his door and his phone and had no response from either. Please could you get a key so we can check up on him?"

"Well, actually", she replied "that's not possible within our policy."

"What do you mean, 'your policy'?"

"I've checked his file and it says his key worker was in phone contact only yesterday morning and reported that Alex was 'fine', so we are not allowed to intervene within a 48-hour period after that."

"But – you're joking, surely? Alex was with us yesterday, but was anything other than fine after what he did. His Care Co-ordinator, Chris, suggested he come back here so surely you have been keeping an eye on him anyway?"

"I don't understand – what did he do?"

"You must know? He nearly killed himself and spent Friday in hospital under observation!!"

The look on her face said it all – they had not been told. She turned back to the office and came back with some keys. She knocked on your door and then after no response, opened it up.

And there you were.

We both screamed "Alex!!" together.

We could see your body, prostrate on the floor at the end of the bed.

We both ran towards you, and as I pulled and tugged at the thing round your neck, she felt your pulse. We could tell it was too late, but still I ran into the kitchen area for some scissors to cut that thing off your neck. I can see it now – thin blue plastic, turquoise again, held tight around your neck by a wooden spoon. There were purple marks on your skin, and a bit of liquid oozing from your mouth.

"ALEX" I thought I had shouted, but I made no sound – I'd said it only to myself.

By now my horror had dissolved into racking sobs, and the staff member pulled me up saying "We need to leave now, Mrs Holt, I've called the police."

And so there it was. Seven and a half years since you first nearly managed to end your life, you had now achieved it – 1st June 2006 to 16th December 2013. The coroner's report would later state your date of death as 17th December, the day we found you. But you were wearing the same clothes that you left our house in, so I believe you died the night before.

Back in the office they asked me who they should ring to sit with me while they sorted things out – my husband? No, he was of course out of town. What a dreadful task to ask of any friend, but settled on Dinah, who arrived about half an hour later. Meanwhile, I asked them to let Sheffield Mind know that I would not make my 10 o'clock meeting. This was to be interviews for a new CEO – how ironic was that? The police suggested we retire to a private room to discuss what had happened. The policeman who interviewed me was great. I remember thinking afterwards 'how do they do it?' - presumably seeing people in my state quite regularly, and yet managing to convey successfully their concern and empathy.

"Mrs Holt. I'm so sorry. But we've had a look at Alex now, and it's quite clear what happened. Can I ask you why there was a pair of scissors by his head?"

"I was trying to cut away the ..."

He interrupted "OK – we thought so, but I had to ask. I know how dreadful this must be but we found a book in his bedside cabinet on ways of killing yourself. The way he chose was clearly the most pain-free – I thought you should know. When you're ready you're free to go now" he said, looking at Dinah.

"Yes" she said, "I'll make sure she gets home safely."

So – I got back in the car as if it was any other day, and drove home on autopilot, with Dinah behind me. By this time it seemed like my brain had shut down somewhat.

"Do you know where Andy is?" enquired Dinah as we entered the kitchen. "Yes, he's up in Grange, tidying the garden. I'm not going to ring him though. He's coming home tonight anyway, so I'll wait to tell him then. I don't want him driving all that way on the motorway with this on his mind."
"But you'll ring Matthew though?" she continued.
"Yes, I'll do that now...."
"OK, I'll make a cup of tea while you do."
Typically, though, Matthew's phone was on voicemail. By now it was the middle of the day and he could be in lectures – he was in London studying for a master's degree in music technology. I left a message for him to ring me urgently.
"I'll sit with you till you get through to him." Dinah said as we sat round the kitchen table drinking our tea.

The whole situation was beginning to feel like a scene on the TV, with me observing, rather than being part of it. By now I was all cried out for a while and just felt stunned, completely blank and empty. I can't keep Dinah here all afternoon, I need to be busy, I thought.
"No, you've taken long enough out of your day already – thank you. I think I'll get started on letting people know. If I speak to Lynne from Whiteley Wood Road she may come round if she's free, and maybe you could let Jackie know what's happened? Oh, and the Tuesday night tennis set – I'm supposed to be playing tonight, but I can't remember who with?"
"Yes, I'll see to all that. Are you sure you'll be all right?"
"Yes, I've got lots of people I need to tell."
A hug, and then she was gone.

Where would I start? With a list. Ridiculous that in this situation, pen and paper to hand, I was planning how to organise my calls. Identify a single contact in each family/friendship group – like a telephone tree – I decided. I assumed Dad would inform his side of the family, and I would have to wait till evening to contact my sister in New Zealand because of the time difference. I'd ask her to let other family members know. So, just friendship groups then. Once I'd narrowed it down there was, in fact, not much to do. Dinah would be letting all my tennis friends know. My Leeds-based friends and former colleagues could wait, so it just came down to: Book Group/Art Group – they overlapped so one contact would suffice; former neighbours from Whiteley Wood Road – I'd ring Lynne; friends from Liverpool – I knew Sue would be devastated, she'd watched Alex grow up; and old school friends – I'd ring Hilary. There was also Steve and Anne, but I thought I'd leave them till later also. My task didn't last long. In each case it was just "Hello... I'm just letting you know that Alex is dead...." wait for horrified gasp etc... "He killed himself overnight in his flat." It sounded terribly harsh, but what else could I say? And what could they say? I would have been aghast to receive such a phone call out of the blue, but I couldn't think how else to do it. Lynne was out when I spoke to her, but said she would call round on her way home.

Next job – ring the church. This was more familiar territory, as I'd done this twice previously with Mum and then Dad. I rang the church office and explained the situation. The vicar – a very new one, he'd only started a couple of weeks ago, so I'd never met him - was otherwise engaged, but they said he would call back later.

Jobs done, what now? I tried Matthew again, but no joy. I realised then that I was hungry. I hadn't eaten anything all day and it was now nearly teatime. I was just finishing some cheese on toast when the phone rang.

"Hi, just ringing to let you know that I won't be back till tomorrow now. There was more to do than I thought" – it was Dad, sounding very cheerful.

"Well, I'd rather you come home tonight really. You can do some more another time" I replied, trying to think of a reason to give other than the real one.

"What do you mean? What's the problem – we're not doing anything are we?" he insisted.

"No, but..."

"But what?", exasperated.

"OK – it's Alex...."

"What do you mean?!!", alarmed.

"He's done the deed."

Silence at the other end, then...

"Not another overdose?" he queried, with dread in his voice.

"No, but I'm afraid we've lost him anyway." I hated saying this and even more hearing his response -

"Oh no, no ..."

"I found him in his flat this morning."

.Silence again, so I kept on talking...

"I think you need to find someone to talk to about this before you set off home, so you can calm down a bit. Can you think of anyone?"

A bit of a delay, then "Yes – Rex – I'll go and see Rex and Joyce. They met him a few times didn't they?"

"Yes, they did. OK, will you ring me later before you set off?"

"Yes."

"Take really good care driving, love. Stop if you need to."

And that was it. I still had Matthew to tell though.

Shortly after this, Lynne arrived. She'd been there about an hour when I thought I'd better try Matthew again. It was gone 6 o'clock and there was already limited time for him to get across London for a train to Sheffield that evening. I printed off the schedule – there were two or three he could get, the last one around 10.30pm. This time he answered.

"Hi Matthew. Everything OK?" I enquired, as normally as possible.

"Yes, I've just got in – was about to ring you back."

"Is anyone in the house with you?"

"Er, no, I don't think so. Why?"

"Because I have some really bad news. It's Alex...."

"What's happened?" He interrupted, almost shouted.

"I'm afraid we've lost him this time" I said, as gently as I could.

I shut my eyes tight and wished I could do the same with my ears as I heard the snuffling, sobbing noises coming down the line. You clearly could not speak so I took charge.

"I'm sorry Matthew – I wish I hadn't needed to tell you over the phone. Don't try to speak now. If there is anyone you can go and see, close to home, try and get hold of them. It would be good to talk to somebody about this. I'll text you the train times back to Sheffield this evening – the last one is 10.30pm. Give me a ring back when you are able. Love you."

"Oh dear" Lynne volunteered "The poor lad. I hope he'll be all right?"

"He sounded terrible. If he doesn't ring back in the next half hour I'll ring him again."

After half an hour he rang back. He'd found a friend at home, who lived round the corner, and who had helped calm him down and review the train situation. He said he would get the last train, changing at Doncaster, but I said we'd pick him up from there rather than waiting for the connection.

Shortly after that there was a call from Dad saying he was just leaving Rex and Joyce's, and would be home in a couple of hours. Then a text from Jackie saying she would be round in about an hour. So I sent Lynne on her way, explaining that Jackie would be here soon, and Andy shortly after. We had, in any case, agreed that she would provide the buffet for the funeral. She had her own catering business and had only recently provided food for my 60th birthday party in the summer. This would be a rather different occasion for both of us.

As she was leaving the phone rang again – so much communication necessary at this time....

"Hello. I'm Neil Bowland, the new vicar. I've heard of your sad news, Mrs Holt, and I'm so sorry. I could come round now, if that would be convenient?"

"Hello – we haven't met yet, have we, but thank you for getting back. Would you be able to come over tomorrow, as I'm just waiting for my husband to arrive home now, and then we need to pick up our younger son from the London train later?"

"Of course. Would 11 o'clock be OK?"

"Yes, that would be fine thank you. We'll see you then."

When Jackie arrived it took me an hour or so to relate all the events of the day, and the weekend leading up to it. Then there was a key in the door and Dad was coming down the hall. Neither of us said anything, we just hugged, while Jackie quietly let herself out. We sat on the sofa for what seemed ages, holding on to one another, each relaying our side of the story, very slowly. It seems Rex and Joyce had been rather overwhelmed by Dad's sudden appearance, and news. Fortunately, their daughter Carole was also there and was able to take charge and offer Dad some sympathy and support. I explained that we would be picking up Matthew from Doncaster at 12.40am. I gave him a concise – and not too exact – description of finding you that morning, shortly after which I felt a sudden wave of nausea rise up from nowhere and dashed to the cloakroom. Having eaten fairly little during the day, not much of substance actually came up but the retching was still significant, and came from deep down. I remember thinking that the nausea often associated with such shocking occurrences on TV and in films was probably well-founded – although I couldn't work out why it had taken the best part of twelve hours. Delayed reaction?

I'd never been to Doncaster station at that time of night before – it was rather desolate, even in spite of the situation. However I was surprised by just how many people disembarked at that ungodly hour. Matthew stumbled out of the train, seemingly overwhelmed by his large back-pack, and fell into Dad's arms. For at least a minute or two I watched them hugging, both with tears streaming down, thinking what a connection they still had in such circumstances, while having such different temperaments and views on the world in general. I also remember thinking that our family was only three now.

The next morning we all arose fairly late. It was 18th December, a week before Christmas, and none of us felt like it at all. How were we going to get through this? I had woken up very early considering how late we'd gone to bed, and it had taken a minute or two for my brain to register our tragically different circumstances. The recollection felt like a hammer blow, and I was to learn that this painful reaction would be re-enacted every morning for the weeks and months to come. But I stayed in bed anyway, reflecting on the anticipated vicar's visit, and recalling who was still on the list for being informed about you. I realised with absolute certainty that I could no longer relay this awful news to anyone else – Dad would have to complete the process. That day and the next few, of course, we received lots of messages, via all channels, from many people. I had a call from Chris, your Care Co-ordinator, conveying his condolences and offering support from the team for the family. I thanked him but was not minded to consider support from them as helpful. I could not get out of my head the fact that he had suggested you return to your flat that evening – only four days after the most recent attempt on your life –

without immediately lining up your key worker back at Beaufort Road to be 'on your case'. Even worse, a few days later we received a letter and thick report from the Health and Social Care Trust – the outcome of the 'Serious Case Review' into your previous attempt last June. Interestingly, we had forgotten all about it as it was so delayed, but found it more than ironic that it had taken nearly six months to compile as a prelude, supposedly, to avoiding such risks in the future – only to find that they had 'missed the boat'. However, as far as we were concerned, the Trust, and all associated with it, was a thing of the past. Our concern for the future was to work out how to face it without you.

Many people said, or intimated in their cards, "at least Alex is in peace now, after all his suffering." Yes. We'd heard that and probably thought that, ourselves before – but in relation to elderly relatives who had enjoyed a reasonably long and normal life before any suffering. But you were only thirty. And for at least the last ten years you were troubled by vicious voices and untold anxieties. At seventeen or eighteen your life should have been unfolding and developing into what you hoped for. Instead all your aspirations were dashed and you were unable to find a way through your affliction. Everyone always says that it is unnatural for parents to 'bury their children'. It is, but I also kept thinking how it wasn't fair. I was sixty. I'd had a good life so far – with ups and downs of course – but I'd been able to fulfil many of my life's ambitions and had been looking forward to you and Matthew fulfilling yours. Instead, in late adolescence – on the threshold of your life – you were sabotaged, prevented from even reaching adulthood in a reasonable manner. There are lots of old films where you see the main character faced with some sort of threat or annihilation, responding by saying something like "Take me, please, instead of him/her." I now understood that sentiment. I felt that if we had to have a fatal injection of bad health in the family, why could it not have been me at sixty, rather than you at twenty? And that's the worst thing about it. Justice has nothing to do with it. You did not deserve the hand you were dealt – as is the case with the suffering of many people – born with disabilities, or in abject poverty or war zones. But what made it worse was that you were brought up in an environment, along with your friends, where anything seemed possible – but those possibilities suddenly started to fade into the distance, to the extent that you could not see a way to get there – wherever you wanted to be – anymore.

So, my belief in Christianity, always a little shaky, was to be severely tested, possibly fatally, but not by our new vicar. Neil was fantastic. This was to be his first funeral at St John's, and we had not met him before, but he related really well to us and our situation and helped us to agree on the content of the funeral service. He showed a little anxiety when the final musical piece we chose was 'Sweet Child of Mine' by Guns 'n Roses. He hadn't heard of it but their name created worries about the possible lyrics, and so he went home to listen to it, just to be on the safe side. He was particularly deft at fielding what was obviously Dad's and Matthew's scepticism of anything 'church-ish'. The bad news was that we had to wait until 2nd January for the service. We would spend Christmas 'in limbo'.

Meanwhile, we were overwhelmed with support from friends: home-cooked food in the porch, food in the post, lovely cards and messages. My friend Hilary arranged to come up from Surrey for a few days around the time of the funeral. Matthew's friend Ethan was going to come down from his parents in Scotland to support Matthew, and the rest of his friends organised an overnight trip to our house in Grange for New Years' Eve.

But not everything felt positive. When Ethan arrived, he and Matthew went on walkabout in Sheffield to see your old friends to check they knew about the funeral. Matthew had posted the information on Facebook, but had only received three responses: from 'the other Alex Holt' (who you had been friendly with throughout secondary school but had not seen for years since you had some kind of contretemps at sixteen), from your old friend Tom, who said he couldn't go to the funeral as he was travelling to Ireland for New Year, and Richard Jones – probably your best friend – the one you lived with for a while – who was devastated. But there were three other old school-friends who lived locally and Matthew could not understand why he had not heard from them. So, one very wet and windy night, he and Ethan set off to see them. They returned a couple of hours later, absolutely drenched and rather depressed. It seems they had seen Andy, Ben and Joe – who had spent countless hours at our house over the years, with one having a holiday with us – and none were intending to go to the funeral, or even showed much concern or sympathy. Apparently, Ethan had had to take over much of the communication with them as Matthew was too upset by their reaction. I assume that you will have displayed some strange behaviour to them over the years, since your illness, but surely they would know it was not the real you, and should have some concern over your demise – and sympathy for Matthew's loss? This was a really painful under-current to the general air of good will.

Contrast that with the reaction of your other friends, who did come to the funeral, or, if they were away, joined us to scatter your ashes at Burbage Rocks and share a meal afterwards. Particularly moving was what happened on Christmas Day. As you can imagine none of us felt very festive, but we went through the motions as usual, toasting you with champagne, before we sat down to eat. Just as we were finishing there was a knock at the door. We weren't expecting anyone, and I was astonished to open the door to find the 'other Alex Holt' there. We hadn't seen him for about thirteen or fourteen years, and there he was, on Christmas Day, with a bottle of wine! We had a friendly chat, hearing that he couldn't come to the funeral because he was accompanying his fiancée to visit her parents over New Year, and learning what he had been up to since we last saw him. It was so thoughtful of him, and I suspect part of why he made the effort was because we remembered his mum having mental health issues and that during the period the Alexes were friendly she did in fact attempt to take her own life once. And I remember thinking afterwards that I had actually spent Christmas with Alex Holt! It meant a lot.

That was not all. His mum came to the funeral, and made herself known to us afterwards. The church was packed, and I was unable to take in the full range of people who were present, but reviewing the forms left in the pews afterwards,

I found that Ruth, Alan, Richard and Owen – from my team at Leeds University, those who regularly saw you when you visited my office – had been there, but did not come to the house afterwards. I was very surprised, because although the others all lived in Yorkshire, Owen had recently taken a new job in Dundee, and it seems that he had come down the day before to stay with Ruth and Alan and come down with them. They would no doubt remember being aghast when I returned to work after your first suicide attempt, and told them what had happened. Another surprise was seeing the former Music Director who had been your choirmaster but had left St John's for a church in Bristol about seven or eight years previously. We assumed that he was in Sheffield for the holiday, but not so – Neil told us he had come up especially for the funeral, which we thought was rather touching. And you will remember Michael, former vicar at St. John's who had also known you well because of the choir, – he came too, although he was still based locally in Yorkshire.

I hope you would have appreciated the choice of music and other inputs we chose for your funeral. Your best friend, Richard J, told us afterwards he thought it was absolutely appropriate. As Dad, Matthew and I entered the church, there was an extract from one of the choir anthems that had been recorded, one in which you sang the solo. Matthew was first up with his tribute. At first it seemed touch and go whether he'd be able to do it. He stood silent at the lectern for what seemed an age, trying to control his feelings, but just as Neil was looking to intervene, he started, and he had some lovely things to say – I wish you could have heard them. Once it was over, though, he dissolved into tears as, back in the pew, Ethan put his arm around his shoulders.

Meanwhile, as anticipated, Dad was completely wrecked – he had advised in advance that he would not be able to deliver any kind of tribute, so it was agreed that I would do it, and that Hilary would stand with me for support, able to finish it off for me if I faltered. As it happened, I managed to get through till the penultimate sentence before my feelings started to tell. But, by then, Dad had managed to get up and join us, and so it felt right that he was there with me as I pronounced the final goodbye. At the end we had wanted something relevant to you but also uplifting, and so we all filed out to the strains of Guns 'n Roses and 'Sweet Child of Mine'. And this was a particularly significant piece of music for you – there had been a two-year period in your late teens when we would regularly hear you upstairs in your room playing this song, note-perfect, on your electric guitar, with Richard J accompanying you on the drums.

Alex

St John''s Church, Ranmoor

2 January 2014

Alex had a cruel and debilitating illness. Thank you to friends and family for the support you have given – to him in struggling with his illness, and to us in helping to care for him. Also thanks to those in the mental health services in Sheffield who tried to keep him safe and make him better.

Alex was diagnosed with schizophrenia in June 2006, when he returned home from Leeds University saying he couldn't cope any more. Since then, though, he told us he started hearing sinister voices in his head from the age of 15, so he spent half his life troubled in a way we cannot imagine. But in the last few years we have had many conversations with him about happier times.

He really liked to talk about our family holidays. Which did he enjoy most? Was it the long journeys across the Alps by different routes to get to and from Corsica, with Eurocamp, or America – seeing New York, the Rockies national parks and California? Or skiing trips to Valmorel and Meribel, where he, Matthew and Andy liked to berate me for being so slow and cautious? But then he would say he loved all those half-term visits to the Lake District, staying with his Gran, whom he loved to bits.

But he said that the last time he was truly happy was while working in the lighting department at John Lewis for a few months, saving up for his gap year in Australia.

Alex was a bright and intelligent boy and young man. He was gentle, kind and sensitive. He loved animals and so took charge of a number of Holt cats over the years. His favourite birthday treat was a trip to Chester Zoo.

He was quite shy, so was not usually the one with a lot to say with family and friends. But he had a wonderful sense of humour, and – as he grew older – he developed a sharp wit which could make people laugh so easily, but which was, occasionally, rather too close to the bone.

He was also very laid back, which led one of our friends, on hearing he would be studying philosophy at university, to say "well that's good – he can do that lying down." Yet at the same time he was extremely self-willed, so he wasn't an easy teenager, and he loved to argue about things (indeed anything!), often seemingly just for the sake of it – a trait he clearly inherited from his father!

Alex's main passions in life were ideas, music, and football.

He read extremely widely. He was a thinker, and really liked to discuss all sorts of ideas – political, religious, philosophical. He studied Economics and Philosophy at Leeds University but was unable to finish the course.

He loved a wide range of popular music – Elvis, Bob Dylan, the Beatles, heavy metal, Red Hot Chilli Peppers. At 13 he would come home from church on a Sunday morning, having sung choral music at the service, and play Guns 'n Roses tracks in his room at maximum volume. Andy's Mum – and my Dad – both enjoyed coming to services here at St John's, seeing him and Matthew sing in the choir. He played the piano beautifully. He also played acoustic, 12-string and electric guitars.

He loved football from an early age, and played for Redmires in the Sunday league. We remember all those bleak Sunday mornings in driving rain and snow in February, watching him do his best, (often with his Grandad also watching) at left back. Born on Merseyside, he decided it would be a good idea to follow my example in supporting Liverpool, realising that this would probably be a more rewarding prospect than following Sheffield Wednesday or United.

For the last 6 months we had happier times again. On continuous medication for the first time, his real personality was restored – he was calm, gentle and affectionate – and he could laugh again! He had his own flat but spent most of the time with us, so we saw him nearly every day, and shared with him some simple pursuits:

- *cycling around Derwent reservoir*
- *going for a cappucino and a cigarette to cafes in Ecclesall Road, Nether Edge or out at Hope*
- *walking up to the Norfolk Arms or driving out to the Plough at Hathersage for lunch – he liked his food!*
- *and when Andy added BT Sport to our Sky subscription, we were able to watch Liverpool nearly every week begin to ride high again in the Premier League.*

On the day before he died we remember his big cheer as the 5th goal went in against Spurs, and how much he chuckled away at Andy doing his usual scouse impersonation of the post-match comments from the players.

But the problem was that the medication also shut down his mind, and seemed to smother his spark and motivation to do things. Only a week or two ago we celebrated his excellent result in the first term test for his accountancy course at Sheffield College. But he could not be enthusiastic about it. He couldn't envisage a viable future for himself.

So – Alex – our lovely Alex,
Dad, Matthew and I thank you for all the happy times when you were growing up; for trying so hard and so long to fight

your illness; and for sharing some more happy times with us recently. It was distressing for us to see you struggle so, and we respect your decision to leave us.

13. Epilogue – Sweet Child of Mine

I read somewhere that grief is love with nowhere to go. This is indeed what it felt like – a wasteful and painful seeping, bleeding, of a core element of my being. Then my grief started to turn to anger. Anger that you had had to suffer such torture from your dreadful illness; anger at a God who could allow a young boy to grow up with healthy expectations of a fulfilling life only to snatch them away, by degrees, at the very time they should have started to be realised; anger at the pitiful resources available in this country to treat mental illness when compared with those that physical conditions were able to attract; worst of all, anger at myself that I had not managed to get you through somehow.

My continuing work as Chair of Sheffield Mind gave me little hope that the resourcing issue would be dealt with so that services could be improved. In spite of many promises from Government, and the increasingly healthy and open attitude to discussion of mental health issues generally, our Council and NHS service delivery contracts were diminishing through budget cuts. During a couple of years as a Carer Governor of the Sheffield Health and Social Care Trust, I found it difficult to have much influence over improving the voice of carers in the board discussions in relation to service monitoring, planning and development.

Perhaps the vast difference in resourcing for mental illness when compared with physical ailments is demonstrated by our experience of using the two intensive care services at the Northern General, bearing in mind the purpose of these units is to keep alive patients who are at imminent risk of dying :

Intensive Services Unit – Mental Illness
In 2011 you were relocated to the Intensive Services (ITS) Unit at the Northern General from a secure unit in Bradford,

and were considered a suicide risk at the time. The Consultant Psychologist and her team were clearly very able and dedicated, but the physical environment was poor and level of staffing was inadequate. The top two factors which had been identified as conducive to improving your feeling of well-being were long walks and playing your guitar. The long walks were, of course, impossible, because of security, but we were hopeful that your guitar would help. However, after taking the guitar in for you, we later found that, in the space of three or four weeks, you had only been able to play it on two or three occasions for about thirty to forty minutes. The reason for this, it seems, was that the guitar represented a threat of self-ligature – and of course we understood that, even more, consequently! And because of this it was necessary to have a staff member ever-present to keep an eye on you while you played, but that was rarely possible because of the number of staff on duty at any time, relative to the often challenging situations they had to deal with.

Compare that with our later experience at the Intensive Care Unit:

Intensive Care Unit
In 2013, you were admitted to the Intensive Care Unit at the Northern General, while on a Section, having taken an overdose at home, through which you had developed life-threatening pneumonia. You won't remember this, as you were not fully conscious, but you were in a calm environment, surrounded by cutting-edge technology, continuously monitoring your temperature and oxygen levels. There was a nurse reviewing your condition at only a few metres away at any given point, 24-7, with, we understood, only one – or possibly two – other patients to care for. She had the time to take a direct call from me at Faro airport, at a time of my convenience, to discuss with me your condition. We were blown away by the level and standard of care that you received, fully in keeping with the regard in which the NHS is perceived in this country. And we showed our gratitude afterwards to the staff involved – you would have been surprised by seeing Dad tearfully thank the nurse on duty on our last visit before you were transferred

back to the Michael Carlisle Centre, having come through that near-death experience.

Since all this happened there have been significant strides made in both public attitudes to, and willingness to discuss, mental illness as a widespread health concern for our country. Progress has also been made in making changes to the confidentiality issues in various settings which allow for carers to have access to improved information about their loved ones, and enable them to have greater influence and input over the care they receive. As a Governor of the Sheffield Social Care and Mental Health Trust from 2014 to 2016 I was pleased to have a tour of the refurbished ITS Unit in the Northern General. This was, in terms of both physical environment and care facilities on offer, a significant and welcome improvement to what had been available to you. However, the increased public finances purportedly being invested in this area generally are not yet evident to me, and I suspect the Trust was not able to enhance the staffing levels which would make such a difference.

I still feel sad when I think of all those troubled souls that we came across in Sheffield and Bradford mental health wards – some of whom you befriended, and whom we would converse with when visiting you – still struggling to get adequate treatment and care that would give them the kind of recovery rates prevalent in relation to physical ailments. And I wonder how difficult it must be for the mental health professionals who know how resource-strapped they are, and must be faced too often with the tragic consequences for some of their patients.

Coroner's Conclusions from the Inquest, 19 September 2014

Following an exhaustive process, involving interviews with several key professionals involved in your care over recent years, lasting about five hours, the Coroner left us for twenty minutes or so and returned with the summary of his conclusions in the following statement:

Alex Holt (deceased)

May I first say that I am extremely grateful to Mr and Mrs Holt for the great detail in which they presented their concerns to me. I am also grateful to the Trust for their serious incident report into the death which I consider has taken a realistic view of the circumstances surrounding this terrible event.

Whatever the medical issues may be I am afraid that I have a clear view of Alex's history of self-harm. It is abundantly clear that several of these events were very serious attempts on his life. To query intent in this case , given the history of serious overdoses and other harm , would not be fruitful. I recognise that in saying all of this I have the advantage of hindsight.

It is shown to me beyond reasonable doubt that Alex Holt took his own life.

That is not the end of my considerations. I must ask whether there had been gross failures to provide or procure basic medical or psychiatric attention to a dependent person whose condition is such to show that they needed it. I must also ask whether any such failure can be shown on the balance of probabilities to have been a cause of the death. In simple terms, if such a failure had not occurred would Alex's death nor occurred.

A number of concerns have been raised but I turn to the Trust's Incident Report (including the latter point raised by Mrs Holt):

- *The prospect that Alex was minimising or concealing the true extent of his suicidal intent should have been subject to a greater degree of challenge*
- *The referral process to the SORT team never really materialised (I use Dr Bates' words not those of the incident report)*
- *The failure to notify staff at Beaufort Road of the overdose was a striking failure of communication*
- *Perhaps of greatest concern to Mr and Mrs Holt was the failure to provide the type of treatment originally intended*

It might surprise some of those in court that in my view the failure to notify Beaufort Road of the overdose came closest to being a gross failure. But this is not a phrase that should be lightly used and whilst I acknowledge that each of the four points contained a failure I do not think that they are gross failures within the meaning of the law. Importantly, nor could it be suggested that had any of these failures not occurred that it is more likely than not that Alex's death would have been prevented. The test is not maybe but rather one of likelihood.

I shall return a conclusion that Alex took his own life. The court should appreciate that I have noted the four failures and I will go on now to consider whether this is a situation where I am duty bound to write a Regulation 28 Report.

Later the Coroner would send a Regulation 28 Report to Prevent Future Deaths to the Sheffield Health and Social Care Trust, outlining the 'Matter of Concern' he refers to, asking what actions they would be taking in addressing these in order to prevent future deaths, The Trust responded with their planned actions.

Acknowledgements

I am grateful to Scott Weich, Professor of Mental Health at the University of Sheffield, and to Dr Angela Baird, a GP in Derbyshire, for taking the time to read my manuscript and give me encouragement that my story, even with its sad outcome, could indeed be helpful for others caught up in serious mental health cases – whether sufferers, carers, or professionals.

My thanks also go to Hilary Bowling, Juliette de Momigny, Norma Evans, Lynn Rollin and Lyndsay Doyle-Price, for both their editorial input and general support to proceed to publication.

However, I would also like to say that I was pleased to meet so many mental healthcare professionals in Sheffield, too numerous to mention, who tried their utmost to help Alex recover from his suffering, unfortunately to no avail. They need more help from our society to make a positive difference more often.

And I must declare my particular gratitude to friends who gave invaluable support actually during my story: to John and Diana Shutt, who looked after Alex, in our absence, during a particularly stressful incident in his experience; and to Dinah Docherty, who helped me get through my very worst moments.

A Letter to My Son

Lightning Source UK Ltd.
Milton Keynes UK
UKHW011817300820
369075UK00001B/1